Industry Trends in Cloud Computing

David Dempsey • Felicity Kelliher

Industry Trends in Cloud Computing

Alternative Business-to-Business Revenue Models

David Dempsey
Salesforce
Dublin, Ireland

Felicity Kelliher
School of Business
Waterford Institute of Technology
Waterford, Ireland

ISBN 978-3-319-87693-1   ISBN 978-3-319-63994-9   (eBook)
https://doi.org/10.1007/978-3-319-63994-9

This Palgrave Macmillan imprint is published by Springer Nature
The registered company is Springer International Publishing AG
The registered company address is: Gewerbestrasse 11, 6330 Cham, Switzerland

Foreword

It's hard to remember life before the Internet. In a little over two decades the exponential growth of connected personal and mobile devices has contributed to them touching every aspect of our private and business lives. To gain 50 million users it took telephony 50 years, electricity 46 years and television 22 years. Compare that with just seven years for the Internet, three years for Facebook and barely two years for Twitter. In this current industrial revolution, we truly are experiencing a hardware and software technology revolution, the likes of which we have never seen before. As computer hardware has followed the well-documented Moore's law,[1] so have similar incredible growth laws appeared for bandwidth and data storage. Having these technologies underpin the Internet, we are seeing a world where computer speed, storage and bandwidth are increasing almost unbounded, leading to massive technical and business disruption. No companies, countries or industries are being left unchallenged and with that disruption of course comes huge opportunity!

Today the world's top five companies by market capitalisation are all technology companies. Three of them—Amazon, Facebook and Google—have recently joined Apple and Microsoft on this list at the expense of the traditional industrial giants. These amazing technology companies along with many others now deliver their respective software services over the Internet, using what is termed a Cloud Computing model. Introduced as a concept at the turn of the century, this business model is now at the heart of everything we consume from the Internet.

Many books have been written about the technological wizardry that has led to this revolution. However, relatively little time has been spent on discussing the business revenue model variations that underpin the Cloud Computing approach. In this book David Dempsey and Felicity Kelliher bring a unique perspective on the evolution of the wide variety of Cloud Computing models and also where they may be headed in the future. They discuss the need for software vendors to focus much more closely than they ever did before on their customers' success to create compelling reasons for these business subscribers not to leave. They give a fascinating insight into the new world of pricing strategies to attract business customers. What signs of churn should be looked for in the data and what action can be taken? Also, what reasons are causing that churn? All these key questions, and much, much more, covering all aspects of the Cloud revenue model are discussed, with clarity and academic rigour in this book.

Cloud Computing has often been referred to as the 5th utility (joining gas, water, electricity and telephony) and, as we look to the future, all software innovation today is based around a Cloud Computing model. As academics and futurists also talk today about the dawn of the fourth industrial revolution (following steam, electricity, computers and connected enterprise), its transformation will be unlike anything seen before, bringing with it advances in artificial intelligence and machine learning. One thing is for certain; it will be delivered over one of the Cloud Computing models discussed in the following pages.

Notes on Contributors Steve Garnett has had one of the most distinguished careers of any European executive in the software industry. Garnett has been a member of the executive management team of three software start-ups that have each turned into some of the most successful software companies in history. Garnett started his career joining Oracle Corporation prior to its IPO in 1986. He held various technical and sales positions including Director of UK sales, Vice President, European Marketing & Alliances, and was the youngest member of the European management team. He was at Oracle Corporation for 12 years as the company grew to become the world's second largest software company. Garnett joined Siebel Systems in 1996 as Vice President of Europe and a member of the founders' circle. From 100 employees the company grew in eight years to become the world's fifth largest software company with 8000 employees and a $60bn market capitalisation at its peak. In 2003 Steve joined his former Oracle executive colleague Marc Benioff to head Europe operations and be part of the executive team at salesforce.com and he helped take salesforce.com public in 2004.

Dr Garnett recently retired as EMEA Chair at Salesforce.com. He remains a serial investor in the technology sector.

San Francisco, CA, USA   Steve Garnett

Notes

1. Moore (1965) observed that the number of transistors in a dense integrated circuit doubles approximately every two years. In the ICT context, the period is often quoted as 18 months because of Intel executive David House, who predicted that chip performance would double every 18 months as a result of a combination of the effect of more transistors and the transistors being faster.

References

Forbes. (2015). Roundup of Cloud Computing forecasts and market estimates [Internet]. Available at: http://www.forbes.com/sites/louis-columbus/2015/01/24/roundup-of-cloud-computing-forecasts-and-marketestimates-2015/. Accessed Apr 2016.

Foremski, T. (2011). ADP the original cloud company is "bored with the cloud" [Internet]. Available at: www.siliconvalleywatcher.com/mt/archives/2011/05/adp_-_the_origi.php. Accessed Apr 2016.

Moore, G.E. (1965). Cramming more components onto integrated circuits. *Electronics Magazine*, 4.

Cloud Computing SAAS B2B Providers (2017)

As a number of SaaS providers are detailed within this book, a summary of each is provided below. This is not intended as a comprehensive glossary of B2B CC SaaS providers; however, it has been cross-referenced with the top 25 SaaS provider list 2017 (www.channel2e.com).

Adobe Creative Cloud: Launched in 2016, this suite offering is new to the B2B CC SaaS market. It gives users access to a collection of software developed by Adobe for graphic design, video editing, web development, photography and Cloud services. It is built on a monthly or annual subscription service, delivered over the Internet.

ADP (Automatic Data Processing): Originally formed in 1949, ADP provides Human Resource Management (HRM) software and services and is known as the original CC SaaS provider (Foremski 2011).

Amazon Web Services: American electronic commerce and Cloud Computing company, founded in 1994 by Jeff Bezos. Having started as an online bookstore, its later diversification included selling a variety of software, video games, electronics and music media before expanding into the sale of apparel, furniture, food, toys and jewellery. It is currently the largest Internet-based retailer in the world (2017).

Amazon Cloud Infrastructure Services: Amazon is the world's largest Cloud infrastructure services provider (Infrastructure as a Service/Platform as a Service).

Amazon Kindle e-reader: Amazon Kindle devices enable users to browse, buy, download and read e-books, newspapers, magazines and other digital media via wireless networking to the Kindle online store. Launched in 2007, the e-reader sold out in five and a half hours and remained out of stock for five months.

Apple iTunes: Initially conceived of as a simple music player when launched in 2001, iTunes has developed into a sophisticated multimedia content manager, hardware synchronisation manager and e-commerce platform. The current version of iTunes enables users to manage media content, create playlists, synchronise media content with handheld devices including the iPod, iPhone and iPad, stream Internet radio and purchase music, movies, television shows, audio books and applications via the online iTunes store.

Atlassian: Established in 2002, this Australian enterprise software company develops products for software developers, project managers and content management. Best known for its Cloud-based issue tracking application **JiRA** and its team collaboration and wiki product **Confluence**.

Box: Founded in 2005, Box is a Californian-based Cloud content management and file sharing services B2B provider. The company uses a Freemium business model to provide Cloud storage and file hosting for businesses.

Chrome River Technologies: Founded in 2007, this American SaaS company creates expense reporting and supplier invoicing automation software for mid-size to large commercial and non-profit organisations and higher education institutions worldwide.

Cisco: Founded in 1984, Cisco is an American multinational technology conglomerate that develops, manufactures and sells networking hardware, telecommunications equipment and other high-technology services and products. Cisco owns such Cloud-based offerings as **WebEx** and **Meraki**. In 2017, Cisco premiered 'Umbrella', a Cloud-based secure Internet gateway to tackle Cloud and mobile security risks.

CloudBees: Based in the US and founded in 2010, CloudBees is a provider of continuous delivery software services. Initially, CloudBees provided a platform as a service to build, run and manage web applications and is now the hub of enterprise Jenkins and DevOps, providing smarter solutions for continuous delivery software solutions.

Concur Technologies: Co-founded by Steve Singh in 1993, Concur is an American Software as a Service (SaaS) company, providing web and mobile solutions for travel and expense management services to businesses and individuals. Acquired by SAP (see below) in 2014 for $8.3 bn, the company employs 4600+ worldwide.

Docusign Contract Management: US-based company founded in 2003 that provides electronic signature technology and digital transaction management services for facilitating electronic exchanges of contracts and signed documents. Features include authentication services, user identity management and workflow automation.

Dropbox: Founded in 2007 by MIT students, Dropbox offer Cloud storage, file synchronisation, personal Cloud and client software.

EC2: Amazon Elastic Compute Cloud (EC2) is a simple web service interface that provides secure, resizable compute capacity in the Cloud. It is designed to make web-scale Cloud computing easier for developers.

Engine Yard: Engine Yard is a San Francisco, California, based, privately held platform as a service company, founded in 2006 and focused on Ruby on Rails, PHP and Node.js deployment and management.

FedEx US: Established in 1973 and based on founder Smith's 1965 term paper while at Yale, FedEx distribute packages worldwide. Working from a private Cloud, CIO Rob Carter has sought to transform FedEx into a Cloud-centric enterprise (Forbes 2015).

G Suite (Google): Formally Google Apps for Work and Google Apps for your Domain, G Suite was first released in 2006 as a suite of CC, productivity and collaboration tools, software and products. G Suite comprises Gmail, Hangouts, Calendar and Google+ for communication, Drive for storage, Docs, Sheets, Slides, Forms and Sites for collaboration; and, depending on the CC plan, an Admin panel and Vault for managing users and services.

GitHub: GitHub is a web-based version control repository and Internet hosting service. Founded in 2008, it provides access control and collaboration features such as bug tracking, feature requests, task management and wikis for every project.

GoDaddy: Founded in 1997, this is a publicly traded Internet domain registrar and web hosting Company. In 2013 GoDaddy was reported as the largest ICANN[1]-accredited registrar in the world.

GoToMeeting: Citrix Systems spin-off business (2015), merged with LogMeln, GoToMeeting is a web-hosted meeting, desktop sharing and video conferencing software service that enables the user to meet with other users, clients or colleagues via the Internet in real time.

Groupon: Founded in 2008, Groupon is an American worldwide e-commerce marketplace connecting subscribers with local merchants by offering activities, travel, goods and services in more than 28 countries.

Heroku: Founded in the US in 2007, Heroku is a Cloud platform as a service supporting several programming languages that is used as a web application deployment model.

International Data Corporation (IDC): A premier global provider of market intelligence, advisory services and events for the information technology, telecommunications and consumer technology markets.

Microsoft Azure (formally Windows Azure): Launched in 2010, Azure is an open, flexible, enterprise-grade Cloud computing platform to facilitate building, testing, deploying and managing applications and services through a global network of Microsoft-managed data centres. It provides Software as a Service (SaaS), Platform as a Service (PaaS) and Infrastructure as a Service (IaaS) and supports many different programming languages, tools and frameworks, including both Microsoft-specific and third party software and systems.

Microsoft Office 365: Launched in 2011, 365 is the brand name Microsoft uses for a group of SaaS subscriptions, which together provide productivity software and related services to subscribers. Services also include **LinkedIn** and **Outlook Web Access.**

NetSuite: America CC enterprise established in 1998 that sells a group of software services used to manage a business's finance, operations and customer relations. Aimed at small and medium-sized enterprise (SMEs), although larger businesses can also benefit from the consolidated ERP, CRM and e-commerce features. Acquired by Oracle in 2016 for $9.3 bn.

Oracle Fusion Cloud Services: Oracle launched its line of Fusion Applications in 2011, a suite of SaaS solutions divided into four primary service categories—human capital management, CRM, ERP and enterprise performance management service. Fusion can be deployed in a private, public or hybrid Cloud and is designed to co-exist with legacy Oracle products.

Red Hat: Founded in 1993, Red Hat is an American multinational software company providing OpenSource software products to the enterprise community.

Ruby Rails: A server-side web application framework written in Ruby under the MIT Licence. Rails is a model–view–controller (MVC) framework, providing everything that is needed to create database-backed web applications.

Salesforce.com: Founded in 1999 by former Oracle executives, Salesforce specialises in SaaS. It provides companies with an interface for case and task management and a system for automatically routing and escalating important events and products include sales Cloud, service Cloud, platform and marketing Cloud. As of 2016, Salesforce has over 25,000 employees and market capitalisation of $65 bn.

SAP: Founded in Germany in 1972, SAP (Systems, Applications, and Products in Data Processing) is the market leader in enterprise application software. Their SAP HANA Cloud platform was launched in 2013 as the foundation for SAP Cloud products including the SAP BusinessObjects Cloud, and was renamed 'SAP Cloud Platform' in 2017.

ServiceNow, Inc.: Founded in 2004, ServiceNow is a publically traded CC company specialising in enterprise software and IT service management.

Siebel Systems: Established in 1993 and bought by Oracle in 2005, Siebel CRM Systems was a software company principally engaged in the design, development, marketing and support of CRM applications. By the late 1990s, Siebel was the dominant CRM vendor, peaking at 45% market share in 2002.

Slack: Slack is a recently launched (2013) Cloud-based set of team collaboration tools and services. Built on a Freemium business model, users can upgrade to various paid versions to gain access to larger user numbers or additional features.

SoftLayer Technologies: CC and web-hosting service provider, acquired by IBM in 2013.

Spotify: A music, podcast and video streaming service officially launched on 7 October 2008.

SutiSoft Solutions: Launched in 2009, SutiSoft is one of the fastest-growing SaaS providers in the industry with a 97% renewal rate. Built on a Freemium model, the basic version of an application is usually free, while other versions employ a flexible pricing model, to facilitate customised plans.

Twitter: Established in 2006 and a public company since 2013, Twitter is an online news and social networking service where users post and interact using 'tweets' (messages) restricted to 140 characters. While anyone can read tweets, only those registered can send them. As of 2016, Twitter has more than 319 m monthly active users.

Workday, Inc.: Launched in 2005, Workday is an on-demand, Cloud-based financial and human capital management software vendor, targeting customers of rivals Oracle and SAP. Workday launched a successful IPO in 2012 that valued the company at $9.5 bn.

Zendesk: Established in 2007 and a public company since 2014, Zendesk is a customer service software provider, specialising in customer tracking and incident reporting. Zendesk acquired 'We are Cloud' SAS in 2015, the creator of BIME Analytics software.

Notes

1. ICANN: Internet Corporation for Assigned Names and Numbers. A non-profit organisation responsible for coordinating the maintenance and procedures of several databases related to namespaces of the Internet, ensuring the network's stable and secure operation.

Preface

The computer industry has evolved from its early manifestation as a series of technical advances that were used to support and enhance the productivity of an industry or business sector. Today, not alone can technology significantly enhance a business but in many cases it has become the business itself. In parallel to this growth and the maturity of the computer industry has come an equal or greater growth of the breadth and depth of its software product functionality. It now stands as a ubiquitous, sophisticated business domain and as a life-enhancing part of our commercial and consumer worlds.

In little over a generation we have gone from a world where computers were seen as some sort of magical calculating engine to a position where almost everyone in the developed world is touched by or empowered by technology. The productivity and social enhancements brought about by the computer industry have changed how many live their lives, perhaps best illustrated by the fact that we are now on the cusp of the entry into the workforce of Generation Z, a generation who have never known a world without the Internet and all of its social connectedness.

With the advent of the Internet and the empowerment it brings to the connected world came a fundamental change in how business software is both delivered and consumed. Gone are the days where software access and use required the purchase, installation, support and maintenance of traditional, on-premises software. Now the business and consumer worlds have come to expect the availability of their software applications as a service, paid for as consumed. In other words, technology has become a utility service—albeit in this case known by its softer, less technically intimidating manifestation, Cloud Computing.

This book is primarily concerned with the expectation that the customer, or consumer, of Cloud Computing Software as a Service (SaaS) subscriptions is empowered like never before to pick and choose both their SaaS infrastructure and their service provider. This empowerment, combined with the ever-increasing array of supplier choice, means the commercial software developer is now presented with both an unprecedented opportunity and an unbound exposure in this new democratic software distribution, consumption and monetisation world.

At a very simplistic and somewhat removed level, this is the backdrop to this book—a practical examination of the change empowered by the advent of Cloud Computing's SaaS offering and its impact on the revenue models offered and availed of in this sector. Moreover, this book offers insight into the potential of this change to both disrupt and empower an entire industry.

Salesforce
Dublin, Ireland

David Dempsey

School of Business
Waterford Institute of Technology
Waterford, Ireland

Felicity Kelliher

Contents

About the Editors

David Dempsey is Executive Director and Senior Vice President at Salesforce, based at the company's Irish headquarters in Dublin. An original co-founder of Salesforce Europe in 2000, David is currently responsible for the management and delivery of the company's Global Renewals through teams based in Dublin, San Francisco, Toronto, Tokyo, Singapore and Sydney. As the only founding European director currently still active within the company, David has seen the European, Middle East and Africa (EMEA) division of Salesforce grow from a three-person Irish start-up to a pan-European business with 1000+ employees based at the company's Irish offices and over 3000 across Europe. Prior to establishing Salesforce EMEA, David held executive positions at Oracle, in both the UK and Ireland, including nine years spent as Head of Ireland Consulting Services. David is a certified member of the Institute of Directors and has both an MBA (2005) and a DBA (2015) from Waterford Institute of Technology (WIT), Ireland.

Salesforce is the largest enterprise Cloud Computing company and the fastest-growing top ten software companies in the world. A publically traded company on the New York Stock Exchange, Salesforce has a market capitalisation of $60 bn (June 2017) with over 25,000 employees worldwide. The company announced in May 2017 that its first quarter fiscal year 2018 revenue was $2.39 bn, up 25% year-over-year, with full fiscal year 2018 revenue guidance of $10.25 bn. Recognised by *Forbes* as the World's Most Innovative Company 2011, 2012, 2013, 2014 and by Gartner as the World's Number 1 customer relationship management (CRM) company in 2014, Salesforce has been named one of *Fortune's* 100 Best Companies to Work for the eighth year in a row and was awarded Irelands Number 1 Best Workplace in 2016. Salesforce is also recognised by *Fortune* magazine as the Most Admired Company in the Computer Software Industry for the last three years.

Felicity Kelliher has nearly 20 years of teaching and training experience in the Higher Education sector, alongside 12 years of leadership experience in senior Project Management and International Retail and Finance Consultancy roles in the information technology sector. As Co-founder of the award-winning RIKON group (www.rikon.ie) at the School of Business, Waterford Institute of Technology (WIT), Ireland, Felicity works closely with small business owners to enhance management capabilities and learning in their organisations. She was awarded the Knowledge Transfer Ireland (KTI) Research2Business Collaborative Impact award in 2015 in relation to this work. Her current research focuses on micro-firm capability development, and she was awarded a Fulbright Scholarship in 2014–2015 to pursue this research at the University of Missouri, USA. Felicity has published in top-tier journals including the journals of *Tourism Management*, *Business Ethics* and *International Marketing Management*, amongst others, and co-edited a book published by Palgrave Pivot in 2015. She has co-authored winning entries to the European Foundation of Management Development (EFMD) case writing competition and has won a number of best paper awards at national and international management conferences.

Since joining academia in 2000, Felicity has led a number of executive programs including the Doctorate of Business Administration (2008–2015) and the MBS in the Management of Change (2005–2007). As a Senior Lecturer in Management (WIT) and Professor of Innovation and Entrepreneurship (Shanghai University MBA Partner Faculty) she lectures on Doctoral, Masters and Executive programs specialising in leadership, organisational behaviour, entrepreneurship and innovation, change management and business development. She also facilitates executive development/Continuous Professional Development (CPD) initiatives and co-manages the MBA insider action research organisational change program. Felicity is a Minister (MP)-appointed member of the Irish Research Council, a member of the Royal Irish Academy Social Science Committee, and is Chair of the Irish Academy of Management National Council.

Cloud Computing SaaS Acronyms and Abbreviations

ASP — Application Server Provider
AWS — Amazon Web Services
B2B — Business-to-Business
B2C — Business-to-Consumer
CB — Cloud Broker
CC — Cloud Computing
CIS — Customer Intelligence Specialist
CLV — Customer Lifetime Value
CPD — Continuous Professional Development
CPU — Central Processing Unit
CRM — Customer Relationship Management
CSAT — Customer Satisfaction Score
CSP — Cloud Service Provider
DSS — Decision Support Systems
ERP — Enterprise Resource Planning
EVPC — Engagement Value Price Cost (framework)
FLF — Feature Limited Freemium
HRM — Human Resource Management
IaaS — Infrastructure as a Service
ICANN — Internet Corporation for Assigned Names and Numbers
ICT — Information and Communication Technology
IDC — International Data Corporation
IPO — Initial Public Offering

IS	Information System
IT	Information Technology
LCV	Lifetime Customer Value
NIST	National Institute of Standards and Technology
NPS	Net Promoter Score
OS	Operating System
PaaS	Platform as a Service
PC	Personal Computer
QoS	Quality of Service
RFL	Reasons for Loss
RLF	Resource Limited Freemium
ROI	Return on Investment
SA	Service Architecture
SaaS	Software as a Service
SaaS-QUAL	SERVQUAL model adapted to the SaaS environment
SERVQUAL	Service Quality (Framework)
SLA	Service-Level Agreement
TAM	Total Addressable Market
TLF	Time Limited Freemium
SM	Service Management
SQ	Service Quality
VM	Virtual Machine
VPC	Value Price Cost (framework)

List of Figures

List of Tables

1

Introduction

Cloud Computing (CC) has created a new paradigm for the distribution of computer software applications and service (Skilton and Director 2010). It offers a model for delivering ubiquitous, on-demand access to a shared pool of computing resources, which can be rapidly provisioned, released and consumed with minimal management effort or service provider interaction. In parallel with this technical paradigm shift, software licencing and hosted delivery models have emerged in recent years wherein software is now licenced on a subscription, or rental, basis. In this new licencing world, revenue now typically flows into the industry on a subscription basis after the delivery of the application service. This approach counters the traditional or classic software licence model where an upfront and 'in advance' software payment was the industry norm (Osterwalder and Yves 2010).

The implications of this change for the traditional software industry are very significant (Meeker et al. 2010). Altering how software purchasers acquire and fund their software licences means that many existing industry incumbents will be faced with Christensen's (2013) classic dilemma in their need to innovate quickly while facing massive disruption to their existing revenue stream. For the software end user it also

© The Author(s) 2018
D. Dempsey, F. Kelliher, *Industry Trends in Cloud Computing*,
https://doi.org/10.1007/978-3-319-63994-9_1

delivers a new democratisation whereby the levels of software application functionality previously only offered on a perpetual licence basis, at a price point beyond the reach of most Small and Medium Enterprises (SMEs), are now made available on a 'pay as consumed' time rental basis, affordable by all (Seethamraju 2015). As Armbrust et al. (2010) rightly point out, this means that the business advantage these software applications can give now becomes available to all, rather than being restricted to those businesses with the biggest budgets.

Within this new service paradigm CC enabled software as a service (SaaS) has fundamentally changed the revenue expectations and business model for the application software industry. While defined in different ways, *The Economist* summarises SaaS as:

> The delivery of software as an Internet-based service via a web browser, rather than as a product that must be purchased, installed and maintained. (The Economist 20 Apr 2006)

Instead of the industry's old expectation of once-off, perpetual and upfront licence fees, this new software licencing model now brings a renewable revenue stream directly to the software industry (Marston et al. 2011). Specifically, SaaS 'focuses on separating the possession and ownership of software from its use' (Turner et al. 2003), such that consumption and usage are the arbitrators of value perceived and price paid. In this new world, revenue protection, or securing the SaaS subscription renewal fee, is critical to the survival and prosperity of the Cloud SaaS business. Any significant attrition, that is, cancellation or reduction of the service by a subscriber, can have an equally significant impact on the financial viability of the service provider based on this revenue model (Burez and van den Poel 2007; Khajvand and Mohammad 2011), a reality that the CC industry suppliers ignore at their peril.

Cloud Computing has created a new paradigm for the distribution of computer software applications among business-to-business (B2B) clients and impacts on how Cloud service providers pursue, acquire and retain B2B clients. The research documented in this book considers the revenue expectation of the SaaS B2B CC industry and its necessary dependency on renewal subscriptions (Li et al. 2017; Skilton and Director 2010; Turner et al. 2003). Specifically, the recorded study focuses on the revenue attrition risks inherent in the B2B SaaS business model (Fader and Hardie 2007). This is one of the first academic research projects to look at the commercial, rather than the technical, drivers of a world-class CC business. In doing so it creates a focus on the robustness and resilience of the CC SaaS business model and, in particular, those factors which can impact the sustainability of the industry's recurring revenue subscription model.

This repeatable revenue dependency is both a strength and a weakness (Ma and Seidmann 2008) to a new marketplace, which in itself is a disintermediation threat (Christensen 2013) to the classic software industry revenue model on which the industry was founded (Osterwalder and Yves 2010). Influenced by this dilemma, our underlying goals are to identify the unique objectives and characteristics which influence the SaaS subscription renewal decision (Burez and van den Poel 2007) while also considering the subjective influences which inform that decision.

Because of the expected growth and attraction of the CC market (Li et al. 2017; Meeker et al. 2010), there is much interest and aspiration among providers to be part of its growth trajectory. As such, the practical outputs from this book are likely to find easy access to implementation across industry aspirants worldwide, particularly those focused on long-term sustainability. While we believe the research findings exhibited in this book offer a universal revenue protection framework, it is not the silver bullet which will guarantee long-term success for all and we caution that its applicability be measured for its appropriateness to every industry incumbent and aspirant.

The company data and industry insight provided within this text has been earned not only through a long apprenticeship within the industry on the part of one of the authors but also through both editors being present in the commercial computer and CC industries when in their infancy. The growth of Cloud Computing has been phenomenal and fast—so too will its emergent data points be produced and morph at an equally furious pace. Sometimes, the pace of academic research and publication fails to keep pace with the industry it examines so this text seeks to make the latest industry experience available as a set of guiding principles for those CC subscription service providers seeking to build long-term, sustainable revenue streams. In doing so, it is not a substitute for customer focus tactics and we strongly advise that any industry aspirant must also pay close attention to this customer focus in parallel with any pure revenue protection goals.

In this book, we explore the notion of a democratisation of both the software distribution and consumption worlds. Using the historical evidence of subscription users as a conceptual lens, we set out to build a model which supports the delivery and consumption of application SaaS rather than as a traditional business asset. This approach enables us to explore the world beyond that of the traditional software vendor to a new place where software is consumed democratically through the use of online access and interactions. This tactic forms part of a process enabling us to examine the reasons why a SaaS B2B subscriber might be encouraged to not alone initially consume the software offered but to continue to want to use it as it becomes more and more tailored to meet their business values and needs.

The text also offers insight into the B2B SaaS business model and the inherent revenue model and, as such, it should be of interest to SaaS providers as well as both Marketing and Information System educators, academics and professional advisors. To support this aim, the primary research documented throughout the text seeks to examine the drivers behind the B2B SaaS subscription renewal decision and, in doing so, to explore the potential for alternative recurring revenue models for the Cloud SaaS business.

The initial research question sought to look at the alternative B2B recurring revenue models, which might facilitate the delivery of a commercially viable SaaS business through a CC channel. Based on our review of prior studies and evident CC market activities, there were two clear research problems to be investigated. The first was that little clear data exists on identifying the unique characteristics which influence the SaaS subscription renewal decision (Burez and van den Poel 2007). The second was that no literature exists, to the best of our knowledge, on the subjective influences which inform that decision. This is despite calls for research in this area since the 1970s (Monroe 1973) to the present day

(Li et al. 2017). Pursuit of both the objective and subjective influences on the attrition/renewal decision form the basis of this book, which seeks to

1. Examine existing software revenue models and assess their applicability to CC SaaS provision.
2. Identify the drivers, risk factors and subscription renewal influences in CC SaaS B2B renewals.
3. Explore the reasons why customers (subscribers) renew, reduce or attrit their SaaS or CC subscription services.
4. Analyse the renewal criteria applied by B2B clientele.
5. Propose a B2B revenue renewal model for delivery of SaaS through a CC channel.

The text includes an examination of the existing software distribution and revenue models and assesses their applicability to the Cloud SaaS provider. It also investigates the principles of customer relationship management (CRM) as applied to this sector. When contemplating the customer relationship in this domain, we believe that relevant decision criteria must include both the identification of the B2B SaaS commercial end users' renewal habits and their predictability. In analysing the renewal criteria applied by B2B clientele those patterns or predictors which emerged from the data allowed us to consider the subscription renewal tendencies. It also offered us the opportunity to seek out trends or patterns in the data and prior research.

Securing SaaS subscription renewal is critical to the survival and prosperity of the Cloud SaaS business as any significant attrition, that is, cancellation or reduction of the service, can have a significant impact on the financial viability of SaaS businesses based on this model. Pursuit of a sustainable revenue stream can be informed by the insights within this book. This in turn should allow aspiring or existing Cloud SaaS providers to build both an awareness and the commercial exploitation of relevant trends into their business modelling and planning and their revenue strategy.

It is important to note that the research that informs this text does not deal with any exposure resulting from the failure for the CC or SaaS provider in not technically delivering the service subscribed for. Instead, it focuses exclusively on the risk for the Cloud company in not protecting its subscriber base and in doing so seeks to build out a recurring revenue model for the delivery of SaaS through a CC channel. We acknowledge that the need for, and costs of providing, SaaS continues throughout the life of the SaaS subscription contract and that any failure to deliver this service, and its resultant revenue failure, could quickly become catastrophic for the CC company. However, this element of SaaS provision is dealt with elsewhere (e.g. Mell and Grance 2011) and is beyond the scope of this book.

In this work, we explore the many definitions of B2B, CC and SaaS and offer the industry practical learning from a trawl through the potential revenue models that can be adapted by the sector. Building on these foundations and through contemplation of cancelled subscription customer data based on a global CC provider's experience, we help the SaaS provider to both identify and maximise the business responses necessary to offset these exposures, not just the objective facts of the cancelled subscription decision but also the subjective reasons given for the non-renewal of the SaaS agreement. Further, we go on to consider the potential of this subjectivity in its influence on the renewal decision makers' mindset, including concerning ourselves with identifying a means to potentially legislate for this subjective influence through the objective measuring of its influences. Finally, using the subscription renewal event as the catalyst, we also expand on the learning surfaced to consider the potential for using the revenue renewal event as an opportunity for expansion or growth of the B2B CC relationship, particularly as it relates to the SaaS influencing factors identified by the renewal business taxonomy.

Thus, this book considers the revenue expectation of the CC industry and its dependency on renewal subscriptions, focusing on SaaS in the B2B domain. Its value rests on the identification, explanation and comprehension of the drivers behind the B2B client's subscription renewal decision in the SaaS domain and in enhancing the knowledge of the renewal habits of the CC subscriber by building on its own experiences and those of other subscription services.

In doing this, the objective logic of the renewal event is separated from the subjective reasoning of the subscriber decision, producing a conceptual model setting out the decision criteria which can influence the likelihood of renewal (Brannen and Nilsen 2005). Previously there have been several laudable projects that have examined and researched, building resilience into the business models for the traditional computing industry (Bonaccorsi et al. 2006; Chesbrough and Rosenbloom 2002). However, the aim of this publication is that of a more recent and broader remit to support the new CC SaaS paradigm.

References

Armbrust, M., Fox, A., Griffith, R., Joseph, A., Katz, R., Konwinski, A., Lee, G., Patterson, D., Rabkin, A., Stoica, I., & Zaharia, M. (2010). A view of Cloud Computing. *Communications of the ACM, 53*(4), 50–58.

Bonaccorsi, A., Giannangeli, S., & Rossi, C. (2006). Entry strategies under competing standards: Hybrid business models in the open source software industry. *Management Science, 52*(7), 1085–1098.

Brannen, J., & Nilsen, A. (2005). Individualisation, choice and structure: A discussion of current trends in sociological analysis. *The Sociological Review, 53*(3), 412–428.

Burez, J., & Van den Poel, D. (2007). CRM at a pay-TV company: Using analytical models to reduce customer attrition by targeted marketing for subscription services. *Expert Systems with Applications, 32*(2), 277–288.

Chesbrough, H., & Rosenbloom, R. S. (2002). The role of the business model in capturing value from innovation: Evidence from Xerox Corporation's technology spin-off companies. *Industrial and Corporate Change, 11*(3), 529–555.

Christensen, C. (2013). *The innovator's dilemma: When new technologies cause great firms to fail*. Boston: Harvard Business Review Press.

Fader, P. S., & Hardie, B. (2007). How to project customer retention. *Journal of Interactive Marketing, 21*(1), 76–90.

Khajvand, M., & Mohammad, J. (2011). Estimating customer future value of different customer segments based on adapted RFM model in retail banking context. *Procedia Computer Science, 3*, 1327–1332.

Li, S., Cheng, H. K., Duan, Y., & Yang, Y.-C. (2017). A study of enterprise software licensing models. *Journal of Management Information Systems, 34*(1), 177–205.

Ma, D., & Seidmann, A. (2008). The pricing strategy analysis for the 'Software-as-a-service' business model. In *5th International Workshop on Grid Economics and Business Models* (pp. 103–122). Berlin/Heidelberg: Springer.

Marston, S., Li, Z., Bandyopadhyay, S., Zhang, J., & Ghalsasi, A. (2011). Cloud Computing – The business perspective. *Decision Support Systems, 51*(1), 176–189.

Meeker, M., Pitz, B., & Fitzgerald, B. (2010, June). *Internet trends* (Private paper). US: Morgan Stanley Research [Internet]. Available at: http://211.157.29.42/F10Data/HYBG_NEW/DOC/180.pdf. Accessed Aug 2013.

Mell, P., & Grance, T. (2011). *The NIST definition of Cloud Computing* (National Institute of Standards and Technology special publication, 800-145). US: Department of Commerce.

Monroe, K. (1973). Buyers' subjective perceptions of price. *Journal of Marketing Research, 10*(1), 70–80.

Osterwalder, A., & Yves, P. (2010). *Business model generation: A handbook for visionaries, game changers, and challengers.* Self published [Internet]. Available at: www.businessmodelgeneration.com. Accessed Jan 2017.

Seethamraju, R. (2015). Adoption of Software as a Service (SaaS) Enterprise Resource Planning (ERP) Systems in Small and Medium Sized Enterprises (SMEs). *Information Systems Frontiers, 17*, 475–492.

Skilton, M., & Director, C. (2010). *Building return on investment from Cloud Computing* (White Paper). US: Cloud Business Artifacts Project, Cloud Computing Work Project, The Open Group.

The Economist. (2006, April 20). *Software Universal Service?*

Turner, M., Budgen, D., & Brereton, P. (2003). Turning software into a service. *Computer, 36*(10), 38–44.

2

Cloud Computing

2.1 Introduction

This chapter seeks to define Cloud Computing (CC) and charts the evolution of the CC concept. The journey from the computer utilities perspective through to the CC utility delivery model and on to the commercial acceptance and take-up of enhanced technology is documented. The ongoing need for access to more and more powerful computing technologies is discussed and the success of the distributed computing model chronicled. The trajectory to a technically connected world provides the reader with a visual tool as to the history embedded in the current CC offering. With reference to the potential future trajectory, we also offer insight into the primarily industry-led forecasts and predictions for the CC industry's future.

2.2 The Origins of Cloud Computing

It's hard to imagine a time before the Internet. But for those of a certain generation, what's now ubiquitous was once only a futuristic dream. Just a couple of decades ago access to computing power was

© The Author(s) 2018
D. Dempsey, F. Kelliher, *Industry Trends in Cloud Computing*,
https://doi.org/10.1007/978-3-319-63994-9_2

only available to the privileged few—either those in the biggest government or scientific organisations or those in well-funded commercial enterprises. But the proliferation of online access and Cloud-based services has irreversibly changed the landscape both for the commercial and for the personal computer user. Now there is a genuine expectation about the availability of bandwidth, connectivity and computer applications, with no more knowledge required to access this widespread supercomputing power than to be able to use a tablet or smartphone.

As we steered towards the end of the last century, the 'father of the Internet' Leonard Kleinrock (1969, as cited in Leiner et al. 1997) and the original ARPANET[1] team looked forward to the time that computer networks would grow in sophistication so that we would eventually see the emergence of 'computer utilities', where computing needs could be accessed and paid for as used with the same ease with which electricity or telephonic services are consumed. Fifty years later, their dream and predictions have largely come true. While early take-up of CC technology was patchy (Brumec and Vrcek 2013), in the last decade it has begun to experience the growth that Meeker et al. (2010) envisaged. Forbes (Columbus 2017) estimates the CC marketplace to have a value of $162 billion in 2020, equating to a 19% compound annual growth rate over 2015 revenues of $67 billion. It has also been estimated that Software as a Service (SaaS) sales will grow from $22.6 billion in 2013 to $50.8 billion in 2018, with a yearly growth rate of around 17.6% (Columbus 2014).

Many of today's users, or as they should more properly be called, consumers of computing services have no knowledge of or care for the complexities and technical wizardry required to deliver the CC services they consume. Instead, they expect these services, whatever shape or form they might take, to be simply there—always available, always robust and always at an ever-decreasing price or cost to consume as and when required. In addition to this expectation of an omnipresent service, the advent of the Internet has also empowered consumers with undreamt leverage over the service suppliers and service vendors (Clohessy et al. 2016; Pitt et al. 2002) with whom they interact. As never before, and exactly as Mell and Grance (2011) articulate, the SaaS business user now has the ultimate democratic business power.

The decision to continue to use or to drop the SaaS subscription can now be made by an empowered subscriber emblazoned with 'easy in, easy out' subscription choices not available to previous business generations. This commercial clout has empowered subscription consumers like never before. CC providers are left experiencing 'substantial difficulties in their attempts to effectively leverage the transformational business model capabilities afforded by Cloud Computing' (Clohessy et al. 2016, p. 2), providing an impetus for the proposed alternative Business-to-Business (B2B) revenue models put forward in this book.

2.3   Cloud Computing as a Concept

So what exactly is Cloud Computing? The history of Cloud is well-documented and various authors walk us through the technological advances and commercial changes that have helped the industry move towards the Cloud offerings available today (Lavigne and Kavis 2010; Leiner et al. 1997; Weinhardt et al. 2009). Many of these advances will be documented later in this chapter as we chart the evolution of CC. In doing so our plan is to bring the reader on a journey from the origins of CC through to the current Cloud delivery model. From there, we will discuss the commercial acceptance and take-up of this enhanced technology and its service methodology, as it exists today. However, before we discuss trajectory, it is of value to contemplate what the term means in a B2B context.

The National Institute of Standards and Technology (NIST) defines CC as:

A model for enabling ubiquitous, convenient, on-demand network access to a shared pool of configurable computing resources (e.g., networks, servers, storage, applications, and services) that can be rapidly provisioned and released with minimal management effort of service provider interaction. (Mell and Grance 2011, p. 1)

Breaking down the component elements of this definition, NIST notes CC characteristics as:

- On-demand self-service: Users can order and manage services without human interaction with the service provider, using, for example, a Web portal and management interface. Provisioning and deprovisioning of services and associated resources occur automatically at the provider's behest.
- Ubiquitous network access: Cloud services are accessed via the network (usually the Internet), using standard mechanisms and protocols.
- Resource pooling: Computing resources used to provide the Cloud service are realised using a homogeneous infrastructure that's shared between all service users.
- Rapid elasticity: Resources can be scaled up and down rapidly and elastically.
- Measured service: Resource/service usage is constantly metered, supporting optimisation of resource usage, usage reporting to the customer, and pay-as-you-go business and revenue models.

NIST's definition framework for CC with its list of essential characteristics has by now evolved into the de facto standard for defining CC. This is a reasonably accurate and encompassing definition, although Buyya et al. (2009) point out that Cloud as it is now defined has many different interpretations, both business and technical, so any single view is likely to leave itself open to probing and question. In our view, Cloud can simply and accurately be described as the widespread availability and Internet-led delivery of computer software applications and functionality, scattered among a global user base of subscription service consumers. Where the service is delivered from is of little consequence to its consumer, who equally will often have little interest in the technical complexities necessary to support the service delivery.

This does not mean that the hosting technology is unimportant. The reality is that it's hugely so. But as Cloud services have become more commonplace and commercially acceptable, this robustness of the technology and security of both the platform and the service delivery capability have simply become 'table stakes' which the consumer expects as a given. If a service is not secure, reliable and easily accessed by authorised users then rather than this technical weakness being its downfall, the business will fail because the now empowered user or subscription consumer will simply look elsewhere for another similar service, which meets the entry-level technical, security and availability expectations. Ironically, existing CC providers have set a high standard in this regard, such that even a small disruption in service by the larger providers can be picked up by major news sources (Armbrust et al. 2010).

So, while Cloud requires the most sophisticated, robust and intelligent service capabilities and networks, this book assumes that these are met and delivered by the service products and, as such, we will focus only on the software delivery aspect of Cloud. Within this paradigm it is assumed that the technical infrastructure required to deliver a CC offering exists at that level of technical sophistication which reasonably allows the service consumer to access the service in a secure, timely and agnostic manner. This is the level of service that the B2B community has come to associate and expect of any Internet-delivered consumer app—omnipresent, secure and timely.

2.4   Attributes of a Cloud Computing Environment

Several attributes of CC motivate organisations to adopt CC (Lewis 2012; Strowd and Lewis 2010; Rezaei 2014). These include:

- **Availability:** Refers to the users' access to applications and data globally.
- **Collaboration:** Organisations consider Clouds as a means whereby members could work on common information and data simultaneously.
- **Elasticity:** Depending on changing needs, organisations could use, request and release as much resources as required.

- **Lower Infrastructure Costs:** The pay-per-use model permits organisations to pay for the required resources only, and without minimal investment in physical resources. This means the sector is moving towards variable costs, from the fixed costs model. Besides, there are no costs of upgrade or maintenance of infrastructures for these resources in the organisations.
- **Reliability:** Cloud providers have more robust reliability mechanisms for supporting service-level agreements (SLAs) than those that a single organisation could cost-effectively provide.
- **Risk Reduction:** Before producing major investments in technology, organisations could use Clouds, with the purpose of testing the concepts and ideas.
- **Scalability:** Being scalable according to the user's demand allows organisations to access numerous resources.

Based on services provided by CC, three types of CC models are defined: Software as a Service (SaaS), Platform as a Service (PaaS) and Infrastructure as a Service (IaaS) (Lewis 2012; Mell and Grance 2011), as exhibited in Fig. 2.1.

SaaS offers the implementation of specific business functions and processes that are provided with particular Cloud capabilities; that is, SaaS provides applications/services using a Cloud infrastructure or platform rather than providing Cloud features (Frantsvog et al. 2012). It operates based on a software deployment model through which a CC provider offers applications for consumers to use as a service based on their demand (Lewis 2012), permitting a large number of independent users to simultaneously use the same software application (Barqawi et al. 2016).

PaaS offers a technical service providing both a platform and a development environment. It allows business application developers to build their functional application and service offerings on a pre-proven delivery platform, again providing access to the platform over the Internet. It facilitates deployment onto the Cloud infrastructure of consumer-created or acquired applications created using programming languages, libraries, services and tools supported by the provider. Consumers can monitor and control implemented applications and change or adjust configuration settings within the application-hosting environment (Mell and Grance 2011).

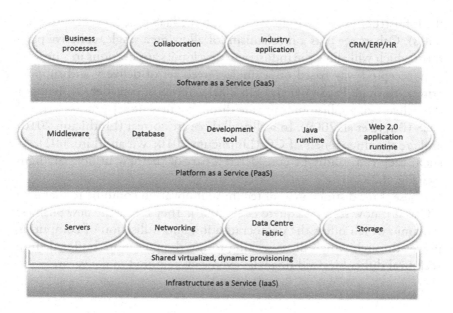

Fig. 2.1 CC service models (Adapted from: Rezaei 2014, p. 14)

IaaS focuses on the delivery of technical, service-hosting infrastructure and essentially provides virtual computing resources delivered over the Internet, again as a subscription service. It offers a capability to the consumer to enable them to perform storage, processing and network activities and to avail of other basic computing resources through Cloud technology. The underlying infrastructure is designed to allow the consumer to monitor or control storage, operate systems and implement applications. They can also manage selected networking components (e.g. host firewalls) as required (Mell and Grance 2011).

2.5 Service Options Through the Cloud Computing Channel

Cloud Computing is something of a catch-all phrase which is often used to encompass all of the many varied complexities of delivering computing services as a utility service. For some it is seen as a means of distributing the infrastructure of the industry through the IaaS model (Vacquero et al. 2008). Others see it as a mechanism for allowing a single, cohesive platform which will allow the industry to develop its applications in a universally accepted way based on a single agreed set of delivery and support criteria through PaaS (Wu and Lin 2001). Yet most consider CC is about the delivery of application software through a new utility process labelled SaaS (Buyya et al. 2009). In reality all three are correct (Linthicum 2010) and are the three tenets of CC (Linthicum 2010; Wu and Lin 2001). As such, each can validly be considered a part of the new utility paradigm (see Fig. 2.2).

These three distinct areas of technical innovation combine to make up CC as it is now seen (Vacquero et al. 2008). They create the new business dynamic which offers the democratisation and utilisation of computing power through which those seeking to use the power are buffered from technical difficulties and financial overheads required to deliver it.

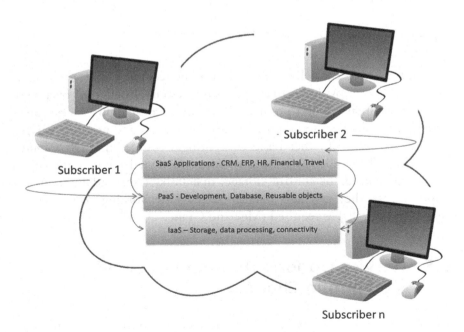

Subscriber 2

SaaS Applications - CRM, ERP, HR, Financial, Travel

Subscriber 1

PaaS - Development, Database, Reusable objects

IaaS – Storage, data processing, connectivity

Subscriber n

Fig. 2.2 CC jigsaw

The core infrastructure requirements are set out by Wu and Lin (2001) as being service time, service quality and SLA[2] commitments (Fig. 2.1), offering flexible sizing in a transparent manner. Fan et al. (2009) define the application software requirements as being lower implementation and maintenance costs, coupled with reduced upfront spend. Looking at the interlinking of these elements, IaaS is the foundation stone upon which the other two (PaaS and SaaS) are built in the CC pyramid. The utility-based business model 'composes services dynamically, as needed' (Turner et al. 2003, p. 38) and is totally concerned with instant and constant service availability. Without the availability of an elastically consumable infrastructure it would be very difficult to create an elastic and flexible SaaS basis for delivery and consumption of B2B and Business-to-Consumer (B2C) applications at scale. IaaS service providers such as Amazon, EC2 and Microsoft Azure make it possible for software service providers and consumers alike to flexibly access software functionality at scale.

It is exactly the same with the second part of the Cloud pyramid. PaaS provides the application service provider with a robust and scalable platform on which they can build their functionality, buffered from the complexities of making their application available to all potential users and without having to consider connective elements. This platform must be sufficiently robust to accommodate the end-user device used to access it, the operating system used to deliver it and the language used to communicate with it. The provision of a single utility platform on which the application can be easily built, rolled out and maintained is a key part of CC (Vacquero et al. 2008; Buyya et al. 2009) and its provision by companies such as Google and Salesforce has allowed the rapid growth of the existing Cloud market (Linthicum 2010).

Finally, at the top of the Cloud pyramid sits the application software layer SaaS. To most CC consumers this is how the Cloud manifests itself. As highlighted by Buyya et al. (2009), Turner et al. (2003) and others, whether B2C or B2B, the Cloud end user simply expects to switch on any device over any network and access any application software package on a 'pay as consumed' subscription service. The level of technical infrastructure and complexity (IaaS) and the platform device and its operating system complexity (PaaS) are completely buffered from the end user through the delivery of the software as a subscription service (SaaS) via the conduit of the Internet (Fig. 2.2). All are valid and full research areas in their own right.

However, the focus in this book is on SaaS and how it influences the business models of the application software industry as provided to B2B end users through the CC channel.

2.6 Cloud Computing SaaS Delivery Characteristics and Relationships

When contemplating CC service delivery, Fig. 2.3 depicts five essential characteristics of CC.

Fig. 2.3 CC essential characteristics (Adapted from: Mell and Grance 2011)

Based on Fig. 2.3, it is assumed that CC resources are both limitless and virtual and the physical systems on which its software runs are abstracted from the user (Sosinsky 2011). Consumers can unilaterally access computing capabilities, such as server time and network storage, as needed, without requiring human interaction with each service provider (Mell and Grance 2011). Thus, service creation relates to the services and applications running on a large-scale distributed network that uses virtualised resources. These are accessed using broad networking standards and common Internet protocols (Rezaei 2014).

This computing paradigm is driven by economies of scale (Li et al. 2017), in which a pool of abstracted, virtualised, dynamically scalable, managed computing power, storage, platforms and services are delivered on demand to external consumers over the Internet (Foster et al. 2008). By availing CC technology, the user gains extensive access to scalable software infrastructure or virtualised hardware on demand (Lewis 2012; Strowd and Lewis 2010; Wang et al. 2010). This on-demand self-service facility is measured by use, based on a SLA. Generally, the SLA includes service criteria such as reliability, security and efficiency.

There are a number of parties involved in CC provision as described above, specifically provider, broker and consumer (Buyya et al. 2009; Liu et al. 2011). The CC provider is an individual or organisation that is responsible for offering a Cloud service. It is assumed that this provider will obtain and manage the necessary computing infrastructure and software to offer services to Cloud consumers via network access (Liu et al. 2011). As CC has evolved, managing Cloud services integration has become more complicated. In this environment, a Cloud broker may be called upon to monitor and observe the utilisation, operation and delivery of Cloud services and to manage and handle the connection between Cloud consumers and providers (Hogan et al. 2011). Lastly, the consumer may also be an individual or organisation involved in a business connection with a Cloud provider who utilises some or all of their catalogued services based on their contractual agreement. The Cloud provider then charges consumers for the services they have used and the consumers have to make payments accordingly (Hogan et al. 2011; Liu et al. 2011). Figure 2.4 summarises the interdependences between these parties.

These characteristics and the underlying provider–broker–consumer relationships are equally applicable to both B2C) and B2B Cloud

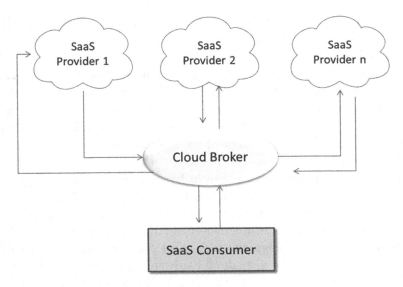

Fig. 2.4 SaaS supplier–broker–consumer relationship (Adapted from: Rezaei 2014, p. 115)

applications. In fact, although often seen as lightweight apps, B2C probably creates more technical complexity for the service provider than do the more functionally complex B2B applications. For most B2C service providers, this is most notable in the complexities of scale delivery where the service is being accessed by many more times the number of subscribers than that of a commercial B2B service. Building or accessing the infrastructure to support and scale to this level of access is both costly and complex for the provider. However, the issues of technical infrastructure and its associated cost are not what this book is about.

We acknowledge these criteria are a vital part of the Cloud service world but assume that for the audience of this book the technical capabilities of service provision and maintenance have already been, and continue to be, successfully addressed elsewhere (Buyya et al. 2009; Mell and Grance 2011). For this reason, our focus is only on the commercial interaction of the SaaS provider with its application subscribers rather than the technical interactions between the two, particularly as it relates to the commercial expectation of the renewal of the software subscription among a B2B cohort. Under this mantel, CC is a model for delivering ubiquitous, on-demand access to a shared pool of computing resources, which can be rapidly provisioned and released with minimal management effort or service provider interaction.

2.7 Cloud Computing Software as a Service

In much of the existing literature around the emergence of CC there is a struggle to identify exactly what Cloud is and where it came from (Skilton and Director 2010). While CC and SaaS have been brandished terms in literature since the 1990s (Leiner et al. 1997; Li et al. 2017), Cloud has only been used within the sector since the noughties, really coming into common use around 2010; as recollected by a founding member of one of the key CC providers:

> It's hard to identify a single definitive source of its origin although I distinctly remember the first time I heard the term used to describe Software as a Service delivery was when Marc Benioff, CEO and Co-founder of the world's largest and fastest growing pure Cloud play Company, Salesforce, led a management think tank in Half Moon Bay, California in 2009, around the topic of being able to very simply describe the complexities of delivering software services remotely to a non-technical consumer audience. Among other ideas, Benioff threw out the idea of talking about the Salesforce service being delivered 'in the cloud'. The idea obviously resonated with the audience, of whom I was one, as it went on to be adopted by Salesforce as the basis for its business service description eventually to the stage where, in 2014, the Company changed its brand logo to its now globally recognised Cloud logo. (Founder Interview 2016)

The subsequent journey from the dawning of a computer utilities perspective affiliate to the Cloud focused on the technical provision of the infrastructure necessary to support the delivery of remote computing services. Once technically established, the CC utility delivery model evolved, facilitating the commercial acceptance and take-up of enhanced technology (see: Leiner et al. 1997; Lavigne and Kavis 2010; Weinhardt et al. 2009).

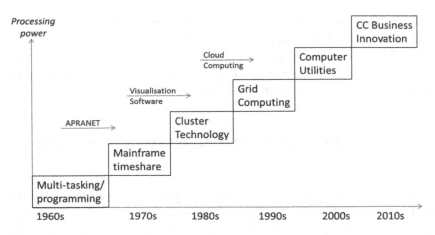

Fig. 2.5 The historic timeline of CC

Over time, the prevailing view shifted to conceive of CC as a business as well as a technical innovation (e.g. Skilton and Director 2010; Fan et al. 2009). Figure 2.5 provides the reader with a visual tool as to the history embedded in the current CC offering.

There have been a number of technological advances and offerings in the commercial technology sector since the 1960s, as exhibited in Fig. 2.5, that have helped the industry move towards the Cloud offerings available today. As technology moved from single to multitasking programming, the sharing of mainframe computing resource among many users by means of multiprogramming and multitasking was introduced in the 1960s by John McCarthy and emerged as the prominent model of computing in the 1970s under its commercial manifestation of timeshare. Similarly, Cluster technology was introduced in the 1970s as a means to loosely connect computers to work together so that, in many respects, they can be viewed as a single system.

Moving forward, from the 1990s Grid Computing can be thought of as a distributed system to facilitate the collection of computer resources from multiple locations to support a common processing goal (Armbrust et al. 2010). In fact, in seeking to create a technical classification of CC, Weinhardt et al. (2009) built on a useful comparison between Cloud and Grid Computing, examining whether Cloud is simply 'Grid' under a different name or if it really is a new enhanced paradigm, which does in fact 'pave the way for a commercially wide-spread usage of large-scale IT resources' (p. 391). CC, in its current guise, has been with us since the late 1990s when companies like Amazon (1994), Salesforce.com (1999) and GoToMeeting (2004) started to offer pay as consumed computing application services. These on-demand software delivery service models come in many forms and provide users and firms with Internet-based access to resources, expertise and an integrated portfolio of complex applications (Benlian and Hess 2011).

2.8 Commercial or Technical Advances?

Initially driven by the computing power-hungry applications predicted by Kleinrock in 1969, the success of the underlying distributed comput-ing model (Thain et al. 2005) morphed to increasingly drive and support the business and consumer applications that have proliferated as the world has become more and more connected. Some claim that for all its innovativeness, it can be argued that CC is not itself 'new' (Parkhill 1966 as cited in Armbrust et al. 2010). For some, Cloud is perceived as merely an extension of the previous technical computing advances (He et al. 2004), as articulated above. Weinhardt et al. (2009), Fox (2009), Armbrust et al. (2010), Weiss (2007) and Boss et al. (2007) also see CC as merely an enhancement built on previous technologies. However, where these authors differ is that the latter researchers primarily examine and view the enhancements that come with CC as bringing principally technical improvements rather than fundamentally changing the business model. In contrast, the key premise of Weinhardt et al.'s (2009) and Buyya et al.'s (2009) findings is that CC is different from Grid and the previous technical enhancements in that the paradigm shift is driven by a genuine commercial acceptance and uptake of CC services. This view is reinforced by Armbrust et al. (2010) who profess that CC has emerged as a 'commercial reality' (p. 2).

In principle, we agree with the Armbrust et al. view of the world and share the belief that commercial drivers are the real differentiators between the technical advances and the widespread acceptance of Cloud-delivered

SaaS as the commercial world has now come to expect. It is our firm belief that Cluster Computing and Grid Computing have now evolved to their current position where computing service provision has finally emerged as the 'computer utilities' predicted by Leonard Kleinrock (1969, as cited in Leiner et al. 1997).

In keeping with this expectation of an always available commercial access to services, which is now embedded in the CC sector, Buyya et al. (2009) refer to this evolution as the 'Fifth Utility'. Computing services made available on demand and paid for as used, similar to the utility model that is applied to consumers when charging for water, electricity, gas and telephone services, is now commonplace in the sector. Likewise, Carr's (2008) perspective that the rise of CC in the information age equates to electrification in the industrial age and reinforces the utilities perspective in context. Carr articulates the move from organisations providing their own power to plugging into the electrical grid in the industrial age and equates it to the current shift from the provision of in-house computing resources to a scenario where organisations plug into the Cloud 'grid'. As he succinctly puts it, 'In the end the savings offered by utilities become too compelling to resist, even for the largest enterprises. The grid wins' (p. 2).

2.9   The Future

So where does CC go in the future? Evidenced by unprecedented market growth to date (e.g. Meeker et al. 2010; Columbus 2017; Forbes 2015; Pettey on behalf of Gartner 2017, among others), there is no doubt that CC is here to stay. What is less clear is how this sector will continue to evolve and how the SaaS offering will manifest in this context. The sector's potential future trajectory and the industry-led forecasts and predictions for Cloud's future revenue and market growth are well set out, with an expectation that the worldwide public Cloud services market will be valued at $246.8 billion by the end of 2017 and $383.4 billion by 2020, with $75.7 billion of that forecast attributed to SaaS (Pettey for Gartner Inc. 2017). The technical and commercial horizons continue to broaden, as evidenced by the growth of the

Internet of Things (IOT) or Data Analytics (Big Data). Such is the speed and growth of the CC industry that these may already be shaping its future. While many industries have yet to grasp the full potential of even the most basic CC service deliveries, the technical and commercial horizons continue to broaden.

This leaves us with a key question, Will the CC SaaS sector continue as is or will it again morph into some new yet to be imagined service, perhaps driven by the data it unearths rather than by the application's intelligence?

Notes

1. The Advanced Research Projects Agency Network (ARPANET) team, funded by the US Department of Defence, developed the early packet switching network and was the first network to implement the protocol suite TCP/IP (Transmission Control Protocol/Internet Protocol). Both technologies became the technical foundation of the Internet.
2. SLAs are an amalgamate of the 'Quality of Service' guarantees when contracting for IT services (Keller and Ludwig 2003).

References

Armbrust, M., Fox, A., Griffith, R., Joseph, A., Katz, R., Konwinski, A., Lee, G., Patterson, D., Rabkin, A., Stoica, I., & Zaharia, M. (2010). A view of Cloud Computing. *Communications of the ACM, 53*(4), 50–58.

Barqawi, N., Syed, K., & Mathiassen, L. (2016). Applying service-dominant logic to recurrent release of software: An action research study. *Journal of Business and Industrial Marketing, 31*(7), 928–940.

Benlian, A., & Hess, T. (2011). Opportunities and risks of software-as-a-service: Findings from a survey of IT executives. *Decision Support Systems, 52*, 232–246.

Boss, G., Malladi, P., Quan, D., Legregni, L., & Hall, H. (2007). *Cloud Computing* (pp. 224–231, IBM White Paper, 321). IBM Corporation.

Brumec, S., & Vrcek, N. (2013). Cost effectiveness of commercial computing clouds. *Information Systems, 38*, 495–508.

Buyya, R., Yeo, C. S., Venugopal, S., Broberg, J., & Brandic, I. (2009). Cloud Computing and emerging IT platforms: Vision, hype, and reality for delivering computing as the 5th utility. *Future Generation Computer Systems, 25*(6), 599–616.

Carr, N. (2008). *The big switch*. Worthing: W.W. Norton & Co.

Clohessy, T., Acton, T., Morgan, L., & Conboy, K. (2016). The times they are a-changin for ICT service provision: A Cloud Computing business model perspective. In *24th European Conference on Information Systems (ECIS), research paper, Istanbul*.

Columbus, L. (2014). *IDC predicts SaaS enterprise applications will be a $50.8B market by 2018* [Internet]. Available at: https://www.forbes.com/sites/louiscolumbus/2014/12/20/idc-predicts-saas-enterprise-applications-will-be-a-50-8b-market-by-2018/#790d296322a8. Accessed June 2017.

Columbus, L. (2017). *Roundup of Cloud Computing forecasts, 2017*. Tech/ #InTheCloud [Internet]. Available at: www.forbes.com. Accessed June 2017.

Fan, M., Kumar, S., & Whinston, A. B. (2009). Short-term and long-term competition between providers of shrink-wrap software and software as a service. *European Journal of Operational Research, 196*(2), 661–671.

Forbes. (2015). *Roundup of Cloud Computing forecasts and market estimates* [Internet]. Available at: http://www.forbes.com/sites/louiscolumbus/2015/01/24/roundup-of-cloud-computing-forecasts-and-market-estimates-2015/. Accessed Apr 2016.

Foster, I., Zhao, Y., Raicu, I., & Lu, S. (2008, November). Cloud Computing and grid computing 360-degree compared. In *Grid Computing Environments Workshop, Austin, Texas*.

Fox, A. (2009). *Above the Clouds: A Berkeley view of Cloud Computing*. Berkeley: UC Berkeley.

Frantsvog, D., Seymour, T., & Freneymon, J. (2012). Cloud Computing. *International Journal of Management & Information Systems, 16*(4), 317–324.

He, R., Niu, J., Yuan, M., & Hu, J. (2004, September 14–16). A novel cloud-based trust model for pervasive computing. In *Fourth International Conference on Computing and Information Technology proceedings, Wuhan, China*.

Hogan, M., Liu, F., & Sokol, A. (2011). *NIST Cloud Computing standards roadmap* (p. 35, NIST special publication, 500-291). Gaithersburg: US Department of Commerce, National Institute of Standards and Technology.

Keller, A., & Ludwig, H. (2003). The WSLA framework: Specifying and monitoring service level agreements for web services. *Journal of Network and Systems Management, 11*(1), 57–81.

Lavigne, D., & Kavis, M. (2010, April). Editorial: Cloud services. *Open Source Business Resource* [Internet]. Available at: http://timreview.ca/article/338. Accessed Aug 2013.

Leiner, B. M., Cerf, V. G., Clark, D. D., Kahn, R. E., Kleinrock, L., Lynch, D. C., Postel, J., Roberts, L. G., & Wolff, S. S. (1997). The past and future history of the internet. *Communications of the ACM, 40*(2), 102–108.

Lewis, G. A. (2012). *The role of standards in Cloud-Computing interoperability.* Pittsburgh: Software Engineering Institute, Carnegie Mellon University.

Li, S., Cheng, H. K., Duan, Y., & Yang, Y.-C. (2017). A study of enterprise software licensing models. *Journal of Management Information Systems, 34*(1), 177–205.

Linthicum, D. S. (2010). *Cloud Computing and SOA convergence in your enterprise: A step-by-step guide* (Addison-Wesley information technology series). Upper Saddle River: Addison-Wesley.

Liu, F., Tong, J., Mao, J., Bohn, R., Messina, J., Badger, L., & Leaf, D. (2011). *NIST Cloud Computing reference architecture* (NIST special publication, 500-292). Gaithersburg: US Department of Commerce, National Institute of Standards and Technology.

Meeker, M., Pitz, B., & Fitzgerald, B. (2010, June). *Internet trends* (Private paper). US: Morgan Stanley Research [Internet]. Available at: http://211.157.29.42/F10Data/HYBG_NEW/DOC/180.pdf. Accessed Aug 2013.

Mell, P., & Grance, T. (2011). *The NIST definition of Cloud Computing* (NIST special publication, 800-145). Gaithersburg: US Department of Commerce, National Institute of Standards and Technology.

Pettey, C. (2017). *Gartner says worldwide public cloud services market to grow 18 percent in 2017.* Stamford: Gartner Inc. Available at: http://www.gartner.com/newsroom/id/3616417. Accessed June 2017.

Pitt, L. F., Berthon, P. R., Watson, R. T., & Zinkhan, G. M. (2002). The Internet and the birth of real consumer power. *Business Horizons, 45*(4), 7–14.

Rezaei, R. (2014). *A semantic interoperability framework for software as a service systems in Cloud Computing environments* (Unpublished PhD thesis). University of Malaya, Malaysia.

Skilton, M., & Director, C. (2010). *Building return on investment from Cloud Computing* (White Paper). US: Cloud Business Artifacts Project, Cloud Computing Work Project, The Open Group.

Sosinsky, B. (2011). *Cloud Computing bible.* Oxford: Wiley Publishing.

Strowd, H. D., & Lewis, G. A. (2010). *T-Check in system-of-systems technologies: Cloud Computing.* Pittsburgh: Software Engineering Institute, Carnegie Mellon University.

Thain, D., Tannenbaum, T., & Livny, M. (2005). Distributed computing in practice: The Condor experience. *Concurrency and Computation: Practice and Experience, 17*(2–4), 323–356.

Turner, M., Budgen, D., & Brereton, P. (2003). Turning software into a service. *Computer, 36*(10), 38–44.

Vacquero, L. M., Rodero-Marino, J., Caceres, J., & Lindner, M. (2008). A break in the clouds: Towards a cloud definition. *ACM SIGCOMM Computer Communication Review, 39*(1), 50–55.

Wang, L., Von Laszewski, G., Younge, A., He, X., Kunze, M., Tao, J., & Fu, C. (2010). Cloud Computing: A perspective study. *New Generation Computing, 28*(2), 137–146.

Weinhardt, C., Blau, B., & Stober, J. (2009). cloud Computing–a classification, business models, and research directions. *Business & Information Systems Engineering, 1*(5), 391–399.

Weiss, A. (2007). Computing in the Clouds. *Networker, 11*(4), 16–25.

Wu, M.-W., & Lin, Y.-D. (2001). Open source software development: An overview. *Computer, 34*(6), 33–38.

3

Cloud Computing: The Emergence of the 5th Utility

3.1 Introduction

This chapter provides an overview of the evolution of the Software as a Service (SaaS) concept and the emergence of the 5th utility. Within Cloud Computing (CC), SaaS is defined as a software licencing and hosted delivery model in which software is licenced on a subscription basis and delivered as a service over the Internet (Barqawi et al. 2016). As highlighted in Chap. 2, SaaS is sometimes referred to as service or application Clouds and offers the implementation of specific business functions and processes that are provided with particular Cloud capabilities; that is, SaaS provides applications/services using a Cloud infrastructure or platform rather than providing Cloud features (Frantsvog et al. 2012).

Rapidly growing in popularity (Columbus 2017; Liu et al. 2011, 2017), SaaS is now a leading practice in the software industry. It operates based on a software deployment model through which a CC provider offers applications for consumers to use as a service based on their demand (Lewis 2012), permitting a large number of independent users to simultaneously use the same software application (Barqawi et al. 2016). It deals

© The Author(s) 2018
D. Dempsey, F. Kelliher, *Industry Trends in Cloud Computing*,
https://doi.org/10.1007/978-3-319-63994-9_3

solely with the provision of access to a range of business or consumer functionality or services over the Internet. This covers both consumer services, like Apple's iTunes or Amazon's Kindle subscriptions, and business services like Salesforce's customer relationship management (CRM) software applications or Docusigns' Contract Management subscription (see SaaS provider glossary for details).

Applying the SaaS model offers Business-to-Business (B2B) consumers the capability of using the provided systems running on a Cloud infrastructure. By using a thin client interface, such as a web browser, various client devices can access the provider's software systems (Liu et al. 2011); thus B2B consumers do not need to control or manage the underlying Cloud infrastructure, such as storage, operating systems, servers, networks or even individual application capabilities (Mell and Grance 2011). SaaS consumers also experience reduced information technology (IT) infrastructure cost, increased operational flexibility and immediate access to new features and innovations (Armbrust et al. 2010). SaaS also benefits software providers through cost reductions gained from scalability and customisation (Barqawi et al. 2016). Based on these efficiency, affordability and convenience gains, organisations, enterprises and governments are looking to SaaS strategies to consolidate their IT systems. In addition, SaaS allows swift introductions of new and innovative software with an attractive payment structure (Barqawi et al. 2016), amounting to hybrid features that may enhance B2B relationships in the longer term (Berkovich et al. 2010).

As discussed in Chap. 2, while some cite SaaS as simply technical enhancements built on previous technologies (Boss et al. 2007; Fox 2009; Weiss 2007), others highlight that it is different from previous improvements (Armbrust et al. 2010; Weinhardt et al. 2009). Armbrust et al. (2010) and Weinhardt et al. (2009) each point out that previous enhancements and improvements have primarily been driven by a desire for a technical improvement, which was also the main constraint preventing the technical enhancements becoming commercially desirable or widely adopted. In contrast, SaaS is seen as a paradigm shift, driven by a genuine commercial acceptance and take-up. This difference is key when contemplating the emerging subscription renewal landscape. It also opens the debate as to the value of the SaaS model to commercial providers and particularly as a guidance as to why SaaS might really be different from the many other technical shifts and enhancements observed over the decades.

3.2 Origins of Software as a Service

While the exact date of inception is difficult to pinpoint, early SaaS providers include Salesforce (established in 1999), Amazon (established in 1994), Workday Inc. (established in 2005) and Concur (established in 1993), among others. All were pure-play SaaS companies—born in the Cloud, although they didn't know it at the time. In the interests of clarity, pure-play describes a company that focuses exclusively on a particular product or service to obtain a large market share. In the past few years, many researchers, journalists and investors have started using the term to describe companies that rely solely on the Internet to distribute products and services (Luoma et al. 2012). Notably, the term 'pure-play' has fallen out of favour in traditional industries and is now affiliated to the Information System (IS) sector and in particular SaaS.

When SaaS arrived on the software market at the turn of the century, IS traditionalists reacted as they have many times before to other similar technological advances that were widely seen as threats rather than opportunities in the months and years following their market entry (e.g. mini-computers; Personal Computers [PCs]; Application Service Providers [ASPs]). This market challenge is exemplified in the following story from 2001 by one of the founding fathers of Salesforce;

> In 2001, Tom Siebel, founder and Chief Executive of Siebel Systems— then the worlds' largest and most successful Customer Relationship Management (CRM) software Company—dismissed us (the upcoming SaaS based Salesforce Company), stating 'there is no way that company exists in a year'. With SaaS in its infancy in 2001, Siebel's comments were typical of the commercial criticisms and market pushbacks that SaaS companies and promoters had to deal with and defend against in those early days. The traditional software industry, then in its client–server phase, was the established 'go to' for software consumers, especially in the B2B

market. The existing perpetual licence business model had very successfully supported the growth of an industry which had built the reputation and fortunes of many of the world's most successful entrepreneurs at that time—people like Oracle's Larry Ellison and Microsoft's Bill Gates, then the World's #1 and #2 individuals in terms of wealth. Truth is, they just didn't see us coming.

Like Siebel, many existing software providers either dismissed the CC advances as being too risky for mainstream acceptance or buried their head in the sand expecting SaaS providers to fade away, just as traditional news outlets ignored the threat from social media in more recent times. Both responses proved to be failed strategies as the SaaS market has continued to grow over the last 16 years, and is expected to continue this growth trajectory into the future (Fig. 3.1).

From a mildly interesting, but easily dismissed, new software delivery model in 2000 to an industry-changing paradigm in 2017, SaaS or its new nomenclature CC, has changed the face of the software industry. CC spending has been growing at 4.5 times the rate of IT spending since 2009 and is expected to grow at better than 6 times the rate of IT spending through to 2020 (Columbus 2017). As Fig. 3.1 shows, the 2017 Total Addressable Market (TAM) for Cloud-delivered services is $99 billion

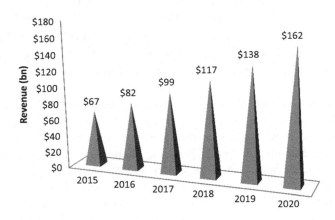

Fig. 3.1 Worldwide spending on public CC, 2015–2020 (Adapted from: International Data Corporation (IDC) 2016)

and is expected to grow to \$162 billion by 2020 (International Data Corporation 2016). The business of software, and in particular its revenue expectation model, has changed forever.

3.3   Beware of False Clouds

There is frequently a lax use of the term 'Cloud Computing'. Many offerings are false Clouds where traditional software and hardware offerings masquerade as the new paradigm. Specifically, traditional software and hardware offerings have different versions of the application available to different user sets as is the case with an 'on premise' or private Cloud environment (Linthicum 2010). One of the fundamental tenants of CC in its true form is the ease of upgrade and maintenance perceived by the end user (Buyya et al. 2009). This is driven by the expectation that any changes, upgrades or application enhancements are made once to a central system with the new functionality then instantly being made available to all users of that application, across all the different licenced tenants who use the single virtual Cloud. This approach 'lets the set of services a business uses evolve' and allows that business negotiate 'suitable terms for its use' (Turner et al. 2003, 38). Thus, single version maintenance is key to the utility business model of the Cloud industry (Luoma et al. 2012) as discussed in greater detail later in this chapter.

Traditional software offerings are not engineered in a manner that is compatible with the SaaS utility delivery model (Lavigne and Kavis 2010) and many application vendors have sought to manoeuvre the CC concept to support their own constrained models while still wanting to be seen as part of the Cloud revolution. This has led to some suppliers offering different flavours of the same product or 'tweaking' the product or service so that it is offered to the purchaser as a hosted solution. This can be via a private Cloud,[1] an 'on premise' Cloud or some combination of these, which results in a version of the application software hosted by the licensee but pushed out to the end-user community through an internal Cloud-like infrastructure. The issue with these 'false' Clouds is that they do not fulfil the 'scale as required' capability proffered by SaaS providers or none of the shared infrastructure of the utility model presented by Lavigne and Kavis (2010). This elasticity is a central tenet of the true CC SaaS model.

3.4   Emergence of the 5th Utility?

At this stage in the technology trajectory, CC, often referred to by its alter ego SaaS, has emerged as the 'commercial reality' proffered by Armbrust et al. (2010, p. 2) and is now being referred to as the '5th Utility' (Buyya et al. 2009). Just like gas, electricity, water and telephone, consumption of this new utility requires the user to have minimal hardware or software infrastructure in their own location. SaaS is delivered as an elastic and scalable service for which the user pays as the service is consumed (Buyya et al. 2009). In the same way as most of Western society now expects to receive water by turning on a tap rather than digging a well, electricity by flicking a switch rather than building a generating station, gas by turning a valve rather than building a pipeline and telephony by using a handset rather than building an exchange network, so too do computing service users expect to access computing power and applications by 'logging on' rather than worrying about hardware, operating systems, networks, security and storage locations (Buyya et al. 2009). As articulated by Diane Greene, Senior Vice President of Google at the WIRED Business Conference, in 2016:

> Public Cloud is where everything is going to run because its more secure and you can benefit from someone else's innovation and focus your innovation on your core competence and there's just a whole host of reasons … you can put huge amounts of data together and do machine learning on them … the IT industry is a trillion dollar industry and if all that is moving to the Cloud it means that there's a pretty big opportunity. We're pretty early in it actually, as big as it already is, we're kinda early in it.

This is the fundamental paradigm shift of SaaS into the utility domain. The technological advances that empower this new means of software distribution made accessible through subscription services (Li et al. 2017) now validly positions SaaS as a utility. As such, SaaS is both the democratic and ubiquitous service that Kleinrock predicted back in 1969 (in Leiner et al. 1997). Just like any of the other four utilities, the complexity and technical infrastructure needed to successfully enable and deliver SaaS must be buffered from the end service consumer such that the subscriber can simply consume the service without any knowledge of, or interaction, with the huge complexity needed to actually deliver it.

The issue with the 'false' Clouds described above is that they do not fulfil the 5th Utility criteria set out by Buyya et al. (2009) and by claiming SaaS status can damage the industry reputation. Notwithstanding the challenges outlined above, true SaaS service provision is proliferating as the industry matures. Initially seen as merely a technical innovation, SaaS has long since moved to become a much more acceptable and commercial software delivery platform (Buyya et al. 2009). In parallel with this transition has come a huge new market opportunity for Cloud-delivered services (Meeker et al. 2010; Morgan Stanley 2011). This opportunity has driven a significant shift of application software delivery to the Cloud as evidenced by the number and value of applications, which the Cloud delivery vehicle now offers.

3.5 SaaS Under the Utility Model: Building an Algorithm of Service

When first presented to the public, SaaS gave the appearance of infinite computing resources on demand, coupled with the elimination of an upfront commitment by Cloud users. The application of a utility model in the SaaS sphere assumes a number of structural and relational supports to fulfil fluctuating consumer needs and resultant service demands (Armbrust et al. 2010). Service fulfilment planning should therefore incorporate an interrelated model of computation, storage and communication to facilitate optimum service provision while also creating a sustainable revenue stream. From a practice perspective, industry providers recognise the complexity of the service offering under the utility model:

> It's not about digitisation any more, it's about being clever once you have digitised … take for example security. I have a friend who told me 10 years ago, 'the Internet is dangerous, you need a fire wall'. He sold a lot of firewall software! Now he tells me they don't really work. So, what we have to do is go from a security mind set where we put out the danger and go to an immunity mind set where we already build functionality that can live in a hostile world … 'We need to become clever with technology. In the old days, we had to build BIG systems, monoliths. (They) had to last forever. The importance of an IT professional was measured by how many kilos you had. You know, what is your Iron (hardware) content. In those days, IT was much simpler as we IT people were the only ones who could use computers. Now, we have more power at home than at work.' (Peter Hinssen, Keynote Speaker, Tech Thought Leader Series 2011)

Based on the preceding discussion, there is a skill in accurately predicting the service required to ensure potential users are not turned away while simultaneously optimising the balance of slack/overprovision when delivering SaaS. Even if peak load can be correctly anticipated, without elasticity resources are wasted through overprovision. However, underprovision leads to lost users, at rates that are harder to measure than overprovision, as these users may not seek to use that SaaS provider again. In simple terms, while cost minimisation is a key objective in the provider company, this should tempered against the reality that a high attrition rate due to underprovision can have a negative effect on the provider's reputation, as exhibited in Fig. 3.2.

As discussed above, it is important to avoid the under- and overprovision of service by SaaS providers, as each is detrimental to the long-term success of the provider in different ways. Thus, industry leaders suggest creating an algorithm of service around these needs and demands, while industry specialists recommend contemplating the following criteria when building a sustainable service model:

- Demand is unknown in advance. In the case of a SaaS start-up, they will need to factor in slack capacity to facilitate a growing consumer

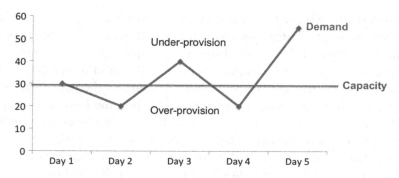

Fig. 3.2 Demand fluctuation impact on under- and overprovision of SaaS

base. In the absence of slack, these firms' reputations could be damaged if service is not forthcoming when sought by the consumer. For established SaaS providers, the challenge of sustained service provision escalates as the consumer base grows, sometimes exponentially. Thus slack capacity needs should be balanced with the running cost affiliate to this activity in order to ensure an optimised cost structure is maintained.

- Service demands vary with time; thus the SaaS provider should plan to have capacity for peak load fulfilment while also considering the impact of underutilisation of their software services at other times, referred to as 'overprovisioning' in the SaaS market (Armbrust et al. 2010). The more pronounced the variation between peak and non-peak usage the more the waste. Notably, few users deliberately provision for less than the expected maximum capacity, so a portion of the service resources are idle at non-peak times. Thus, SaaS capacity planning should include a suite of service offerings available to B2B consumers to facilitate a more even load. For example, off-peak use could be enhanced by enticing usage offers in these periods (e.g. much like off-peak electricity charges). There is an additional goal here as off-peak enticement may alleviate some of the pressure associated with the peak period.

- Service demands vary with user profile. This is an important point when considering optimum service usage as if SaaS providers can target specific industries or sectors in different time zones, there is potential to achieve higher utilisation by multilayering the workload needs of different organisations. For example, those industries dependent on 24-hour service provision may complement a B2B consumer base that is active in daylight hours only. It would be remiss not to factor in the costs affiliate to 24-hour support on the part of the service provider; however, as we progress through the information age, the expectations of users is that they will have access whenever needed (e.g. there are no closing times in SaaS service provision).

- Seasonal or other periodic demand variations do occur; for example, holiday booking season spikes in January while skiing holiday searches spike later in the season. This is of particular relevance to seasonally sensitive clients as these consumers will not need software services for certain parts of the year. From the consumer perspective, the utility model facilitates service provision on a pay-per-use basis, only when needed. For the provider, seasonal consumers are somewhat easier to manage in terms of load prediction, particularly if the service provider can acquire and keep SaaS clients from opposing seasons (e.g. ice cream and umbrellas).

- Unanticipated bursts of demand do occur, for example due to external events (e.g. the election of a new president in the US in 2016 required significant additional resource as users required greater than normal access to follow this news event). While some events can be predicted and therefore planned for (the US presidential election occurs every four years), others cannot. In cases where an unexpected event creates a spike in demand, SaaS providers should have some form of contingency plan to facilitate unbroken service provision.

- Unanticipated service outage. This is another aspect of contingency planning. Using an equivalent analogy of electricity supply, an electrical storm can break service if a pylon is damaged. Reinstatement of service requires round the clock service engineers to work on the damaged equipment. In the CC environment, technical risks include software bugs/faults, server corruption or failure, data confidentiality breach and potential theft of data, cyber or denial of service attacks by service users or the general public. Non-technical challenges include electrical outages, regulatory demands to audit SaaS solutions, a reduction or removal of the service provided, a miscalculation of capacity requirements during peak periods or the SaaS provider ceasing to exist. In such instances, scenario planning can facilitate the contemplation of this occurrence and response trajectory to ensure reinstatement of service in the shortest possible period.

- The B2B SaaS consumer base may fluctuate over time. For start-ups, demand may spike when they first arrive on the market, followed potentially by a reduction in their consumer base once some visitors turn away. This is particularly true of start-ups, who have market entry service offerings (e.g. below cost selling) that cannot be fulfilled in the longer term. Established SaaS providers face similar challenges pre- and post-time-bound or cost-bound market campaigns (e.g. *x* months at a lower price before 'normal' costing is reinstated).

For the consumer, SaaS benefits should outweigh the CC costs. This cost–benefit analysis should include the economies of elasticity (e.g. service available when needed to the level required) and transference of risk, especially the risks of over- or underprovision as discussed above. In terms of elasticity, the SaaS provider has the ability to add or remove resources one server at a time, and with a lead time of minutes rather than weeks. This allows the consumer to more closely match resources to workload requirements. However, organisations worry about whether utility computing services will have sufficient capability to supply these services when needed (Armbrust et al. 2010), and this makes some nervous of moving to SaaS.

Notably, the SaaS industry have set a high standard of both business continuity and service availability, such that even a small disruption is reported through major news sources throughout the world, as was the case with Amazon in February 2017 (Exhibit 3.1);

Exhibit 3.1 Amazon AWS Outage 2017

Amazon's massive AWS outage was caused by human error

Amazon today blamed human error for the big Amazon Web Services (AWS) outage that took down a bunch of large Internet sites on Tuesday afternoon. In a blog post, the Company said that one of its employees was debugging an issue with the billing system and accidentally took more servers offline than intended. That error started a domino effect that took down two other server systems and so on and so on.

'Removing a significant portion of the capacity caused each of these systems to require a full restart' the post read. 'While these subsystems were being restarted, S3 was unable to service requests ... including Amazon Elastic Compute Cloud'. (Jason Del Rey, 2 March 2017)

However, these disruptions should ideally be communicated as a comparison to in-house service provision, managed by the business itself, rather than being compared to a baseline expectation of perfection.

Communication strategies should ideally go beyond the economic, reliability and elasticity gains of SaaS provision. Security is a matter of comprehension in context, where users need to be simultaneously protected from the outside world and from other users. Of course, users should also be reticent of individual encryption policies that can enhance their in-house security systems. While the Cloud user is responsible for application-level security, the SaaS provider is responsible for physical security, and, based on common industry agreements, they also enforce external firewall policies. Providers also mitigate against theft or denial of service attacks by service users. Security relating to the layers of software used is shared between the two parties (provider–consumer) in the B2B arrangement. The primary security mechanism in today's Clouds is virtualisation. However, as with all systems, not all virtualised environments are bug-free and not all resources are virtualised. Incorrect network virtualisation can offer unintentional user access to sensitive aspects of the SaaS providers' technical infrastructure or other users' resources. The highlighted security challenges should be tempered by the fact that these challenges are faced by any large data centre, particularly those with Internet portholes, regardless of where it resides.

Confidentiality is an additional aspect of the B2B subscribers' willingness to engage with the provider organisation on an ongoing basis. In simple terms, the consumer needs to trust that the provider will not use their, often sensitive, data for other purposes. For example, as more and more business functions are held in the Cloud, data relating to a client's payroll, own customer base and research and development may be accessible to the provider. Thus, exhibiting integrity when dealing with a client's data may be as valuable to the SaaS provider's renewal strategy as viewing renewal as a purely monetary arrangement.

Over the next chapters we will dive deeper into the fundamental need to defend the SaaS business against customer and revenue churn, considering both the revenue expectation of the Cloud industry and its total dependency on protecting its renewal subscriptions.

Notes

1. A Private Cloud is a hosted, single tenant infrastructure that, although allowing the end user access the application service as if it were a Cloud Service, is managed and delivered through a single, unique hosted environment licensed in a model closer to the traditional industry licence than that of the Utility Cloud (Sotomayor et al. 2009).

References

Armbrust, M., Fox, A., Griffith, R., Joseph, A., Katz, R., Konwinski, A., Lee, G., Patterson, D., Rabkin, A., Stoica, I., & Zaharia, M. (2010). A view of Cloud Computing. *Communications of the ACM, 53*(4), 50–58.

Barqawi, N., Syed, K., & Mathiassen, L. (2016). Applying service-dominant logic to recurrent release of software: An action research study. *The Journal of Business and Industrial Marketing, 31*(7), 928–940.

Berkovich, M., Esch, S., Leimeister, J. M., & Krcmar, H. (2010). *Towards requirements engineering for "software as a service"*. Göttingen: MKWI Gottingen.

Boss, G., Malladi, P., Quan, D., Legregni, L., & Hall, H. (2007). *Cloud Computing* (pp. 224–231, IBM White Paper, 321). IBM Corporation.

Buyya, R., Yeo, C. S., Venugopal, S., Broberg, J., & Brandic, I. (2009). Cloud computing and emerging IT platforms: Vision, hype, and reality for delivering computing as the 5th utility. *Future Generation Computer Systems, 25*(6), 599–616.

Columbus, L. (2017). *Roundup of Cloud Computing forecasts*, 2017. Tech/ #InTheCloud. Available at: www.forbes.com. Accessed June 2017.

Del Ray, J. (2017). *Amazon's massive AWS outage was caused by human error*. Recode [Internet]. Available at: https://www.recode.net/2017/3/2/14792636/ amazon-aws-internet-outage-cause-human-error-incorrect-command. Accessed June 2017.

Fox, A. (2009). *Above the Clouds: A Berkeley view of Cloud Computing*. Berkeley: UC Berkeley.

Frantsvog, D., Seymour, T., & Freneymon, J. (2012). Cloud Computing. *International Journal of Management & Information Systems, 16*(4), 317–324.

Greene, D. (2016). Keynote Speaker. *WIRED Business Conference* [Internet]. Available at: http://www.zimbio.com/pictures/xh0oHV_bEl_/2016+Wired+Business+Conference/rV4Vq-4GvBd/Diane+Greene. Accessed Apr 2017.

Hinssen, P. (2011). Keynote Speaker. *Tech Thought Leader Series* [Internet]. Available at: https://www.youtube.com/watch?v=7IMfBrBIf90. Accessed May 2017.

International Data Corporation. (2016, January). *Worldwide semiannual public services spending guide* [Internet]. Available at: https://www.idc.com/getdoc.jsp?containerId=prUS40960516. Accessed May 2017.

Lavigne, D., & Kavis, M. (2010, April). Editorial: Cloud Services. *Open Source Business Resource* [Internet]. Available at: http://timreview.ca/article/338. Accessed Aug 2016.

Leiner, B. M., Cerf, V. G., Clark, D. D., Kahn, R. E., Kleinrock, L., Lynch, D. C., Postel, J., Roberts, L. G., & Wolff, S. S. (1997). The past and future history of the Internet. *Communications of the ACM, 40*(2), 102–108.

Lewis, G. A. (2012). *The role of standards in Cloud-computing interoperability.* Hanscom: Software Engineering Institute, Carnegie Mellon University.

Li, S., Cheng, H. K., Duan, Y., & Yang, Y.-C. (2017). A study of enterprise software licensing models. *Journal of Management Information Systems, 34*(1), 177–205.

Linthicum, D. S. (2010). *Cloud Computing and SOA convergence in your enterprise: A step-by-step guide.* Upper Saddle River: Addison-Wesley Information Technology Series.

Liu, F., Tong, J., Mao, J., Bohn, R., Messina, J., Badger, L., & Leaf, D. (2011). NIST Cloud Computing reference architecture. *NIST Special Publication, 500*, 292.

Luoma, E., Ronkko, M., & Tyrvainen, P. (2012). Current software-as-a-service business models: Evidence from Finland. In M. A. Cusumano, B. Iyer, & N. Venkatraman (Eds.), *International Conference of Software Business (ICSOB 2012)*, (Lecture Notes in Business Information Processing (LNBIP), Vol. 114, pp. 181–194). Berlin/Heidelberg: Springer.

Meeker, M., Pitz, B., & Fitzgerald, B. (2010, June). *Internet trends* (Private paper). US: Morgan Stanley Research [Internet]. Available at: http://211.157.29.42/F10Data/HYBG_NEW/DOC/180.pdf. Accessed Aug 2013.

Mell, P., & Grance, T. (2011). *The NIST definition of Cloud Computing* (National Institute of Standards and Technology special publication, 800-145). Gaithersburg: US Department of Commerce.

Sotomayor, B., Montero, R. S., Llorente, I. M., & Foster, I. (2009). Virtual infrastructure management in private and hybrid Clouds. *Internet Computing IEEE, 13*(5), 14–22.

Stanley, M. (2011, May 23). *Cloud Computing takes off: Market set to boom as migration accelerates* (Morgan Stanley Blue Paper) [Internet]. Available at: http://www.morganstanley.com/views/ perspectives/Cloud_computing.pdf. Accessed Aug 2013.

Turner, M., Budgen, D., & Brereton, P. (2003). Turning software into a service. *Computer, 36*(10), 38–44.

Weinhardt, C., Blau, B., & Stober, J. (2009). Cloud computing – A classification, business models, and research directions. *Business and Information Systems Engineering, 1*(5), 391–399.

Weiss, A. (2007). Computing in the Clouds. *Network, 11*(4), 16–25.

4

Revenue Models and Pricing Strategies in the B2B SaaS Market

4.1 Introduction

The customer or consumer can be conceived of as a subscriber in the Business-Business (B2B) Software as a Service (SaaS) relationship as they subscribe to use a specific level of service, normally for a defined period of time. For the purposes of clarity, Business-to-Consumer (B2C) is a commercial transaction that occurs between a company and a consumer while B2B describes commercial transactions between businesses. The literature struggles to differentiate B2C and B2B in terms of possible SaaS business models; therefore, it is of value to further differentiate, refine and segment each end-user cohort in the Cloud world. From an interaction perspective, B2B applications 'refer to the use of computerised systems (e.g. Web servers, networking services, databases) for conducting business among different [business] partners' for the purposes of 'procurement, customer relationship management, billing, accounting, human resources, supply chain, and manufacturing' (Medjahed et al. 2003, p. 59). In contrast, B2C applications include virtual malls, customised news delivery, traffic monitoring and route planning for the purposes of engaging with private consumers.

© The Author(s) 2018
D. Dempsey, F. Kelliher, *Industry Trends in Cloud Computing*,
https://doi.org/10.1007/978-3-319-63994-9_4

As a note of caution, the terms business and revenue and revenue's component pricing are often confused in this context (George and Bock 2011); so in the interests of clarity, a business model describes 'the rationale of how an organisation creates, delivers, and captures value' (Osterwalder and Pigneur 2010, p. 14), whereas a revenue model describes the revenue flow or stream from its products and services. We assume that the revenue model is part of the business model based on these definitions and is the catalyst through which an organisation builds a pricing strategy to deliver services with high margins and offer future funding for the business. In addition to the revenue model, financial targets should be forecasted when creating a business strategy whereby expected revenues and profits can be calculated at an aggregate level for the SaaS provider.

In this chapter, we take a strategic rather than operational perspective on revenue flow (Bozkurt 2016), focusing on the approach taken when seeking and collecting revenue from subscribers based on the SaaS providers overriding business model. There are many models for revenue generation, and the accelerated development of the Internet, social networks and smartphones has expanded these possibilities (Laniado 2013). One assumes this is also true of the Cloud. Thus, the SaaS provider can apply a different revenue model to each CC service and each revenue model might have a different pricing mechanism (Osterwalder and Pigneur 2010). As such, it is worth considering the various commercial revenue models present in the commercial service market.

4.2 Commercial Service Market Revenue Models

As stated in the Introduction, a revenue model describes the revenue flow in a business and the firm's underlying framework for generating sales. The model identifies which revenue sources to pursue, what value to offer, how to price the offering and who pays for it (Priem 2007). By having a well-defined revenue model, a business can focus on a target market, fund business development plans, establish appropriate marketing plans, build a line of credit and raise capital if required (Grant 2004). Without a well-defined revenue model incorporating a clear plan of how to generate sales, SaaS providers will likely struggle to meet a sustainable revenue stream for their business.

We are focused on the commercial service market and assume virtual service delivery, so while retail/e-tail are valid revenue models, these are not discussed in detail below. When contemplating the sale of SaaS offerings to business (B2B) clients, the challenges include:

- Turning a single sales event into a repeat sale/ recurring sale (e.g. generating an environment where a loyal subscriber can emerge).
- Adding extra components to a basic service (e.g. premium SaaS platform).
- Selling a service that bonds the subscriber to your platform (e.g. embedded software and version upgrades).
- Finding a way to price at a premium and target-specific market segments that are willing to pay for the additional value (e.g. dedicated levels of server access in peak periods).
Adapted from: Laniado 2013

As highlighted by Priem (2007), 'many defunct "dot.coms" simply failed to provide sufficient consumer value' (p. 219), so our focus is on 'consumer benefit experienced'. Under this approach, those who choose to adopt SaaS are arbiters of the service's perceived value, so it is these subscribers who ultimately validate the value of the SaaS offering. Despite this central role, consumers have received surprisingly little attention in the business model literature (Priem 2007), something we attempt to tease out in this book. We are also cognisant of the critical role consumers play in the success and sustainability of the SaaS business, so the subscriber perspective is echoed in the outlined pricing strategies.

Based on the application of one or more of the following revenue models, the SaaS provider generates a revenue stream for the company. This is the amount of money coming into the business from the client base. A summary of the identified SaaS revenue models are presented in Table 4.1.

Table 4.1 SaaS revenue models overview

Revenue model	Overview	Popularity in B2B SaaS
Advertising	Revenue generated from advertising. May also be a cost to the SaaS provider	Mid to low; primarily in the B2C domain
Affiliate programs	Drive website traffic to particular sellers	Low—primarily B2C
Auction, bid	Provider acts as an intermediary between seller and buyer	Low—primarily B2C
Crippleware	Client access restricted to a demonstration version of software; linked to the enticement sales model	Mid to low; growing in popularity
Commission	Provider charges a mediation fee	Mid—common model for Cloud brokers
Competition-based	Adopt market or competitor price	Mid
Construction	Revenue model for bespoke systems	Mid
Cost-based	Cost is the baseline from which price based on profit needs is derived	Mid
Data	Mining of consumer data for revenue value	Mid—used to analyse consumer data
Demo ware (trial ware)	Client access restricted to a demonstration version of software (see crippleware above); linked to the enticement sales model	Mid; growing in popularity for more complex SaaS solutions
Digital product	Download and consume digital data	Mid—facilitates version download/upgrade
E-commerce	Purchase products online	Low—primarily B2C
Enticement sales model	Encourage subscribers to impulse buy	Mid–high
Fee-for-service	Charged for use; utility approach	Very high
Freemium	Free for a period/level of use	Very high
Future use	Voucher system	Low–mid
Licencing	Limited by time, territory, etc.	Mid
Mail order, e-tail	Linked to e-commerce	Low—primarily B2C
Marketplace	Like a meeting place, connects sellers with consumers	
One-time charge	Perpetual licence fee, cost of upgrade extra	Mid–low; used to be more popular

(*continued*)

Table 4.1 (continued)

Revenue model	Overview	Popularity in B2B SaaS
OpenSource	Fully functioning version of the software for free use	Low
Optioned	Option to purchase in the future for an agreed price	Low
Production	Customised software generation	Low
Rental	Rent the service	High
Shareware	Make and share copies of the software	Low
Software licencing	Licencing model derivative	Mid–low; used to be more popular
Subscription	Fixed service fee by use/time period	Very high
Usage-based	Pay-as-you-go or pay-per-user	Mid—higher in B2C

As outlined in Table 4.1, the options in relation to SaaS revenue models are as follows:

— Advertising (e-advertising) revenue model: This model originated in the media sector, wherein media suppliers use their platforms as potential revenue-generating advertising space; the potential to redisplay an advertisement which previously appeared in a newspaper can be offered to a customer at a specified cost. It has since become the dominant revenue generator for publishers on the Internet (Kittlaus and Clough 2008). SaaS providers who have an Internet presence may also offer these services on their platforms in the form of text, banners and video, emulating the billboards and television advertisements affiliate to traditional media channels. The SaaS provider is then paid by advertisers to advertise within their software application. This approach does not preclude a charge on the end user. For example, Google and Twitter each generate significant revenue based on their advertising revenue model, having expanded their repertoire to include advertising on apps and mobile platforms.

A subset of this approach is the concept of promoted content, also known as sponsored content, which is content paid for by a provider to promote their products and services within the website content rather than being presented as a separate advertisement. Consumer behaviour research has found that users may give this content more attention or perceive it as more credible than other advertisements (Priem 2007). Some users may even be oblivious to the fact that a provider has paid to promote specific content (Laniado 2013). This model is common on social networks such as Facebook and Twitter as well as on websites such as Yelp.

Notably, while advertising can be seen as a revenue model when a business is selling the advertising space to another business or consumer, it can also be construed as a cost in situations where the company is seeking to advertise their own products and services. In these circumstances, a third party may be paid to accommodate this advertising.

– Affiliate programs revenue model: These models are common in Internet marketing, and include sellers of products/services and parties that drive traffic to these sellers. Some affiliates explicitly state that links to third parties may entitle them to compensation using some form of revenue-sharing mechanism. These programs are used by a spread of providers such as Amazon down to small-scale blog operators.

– Auction and bid revenue model: Built on the principles of the traditional auction industry, eBay is a key online user of this model. The original model applied by eBay is that the price of an auction item is determined in a public auction, and eBay generates revenue streams from a variety of seller and advertisement fees relating to the website. Of note is the recent trend towards immediate fixed-price sales compared to auctions on sites such as eBay, suggesting a shift in user preference (Laniado 2013).

– Crippleware revenue model: In software, this approach restricts program features such as print facilities or the ability to edit or save files until such time as the user purchases the software or registers for its use. This is somewhat like a demonstration model that allows users to take a closer look at the system's features before making the decision to subscribe, without being able to use it to generate output.

– Commission revenue model: This approach is used when a business charges a fee for a transaction that it mediates between two parties. For example, a stockbroker charges a fee for buying or selling stock on behalf of a client. In the SaaS sphere, Cloud brokers (Chap. 2, Fig. 2.4) act as an intermediary between SaaS providers and the consumer. These brokers generate revenue through commissions on the sale of their service or per use, depending on the specific agreement. Transaction enablers also sit in this space, for example, *Paypal* enables payments that minimise risk for sellers and purchase security for buyers, for which they receive a fee.

– Competition-based revenue model: This model assumes that the service provider bases their revenue model on what the market price is for a particular service. The SaaS provider is essentially a price taker under this model (Porter 1980), adjusting their prices based on the ebbs and flow of the market. This is a reactive revenue model and is therefore unlikely to provide competitive advantage to the SaaS organisation.

– Construction revenue model: Sometimes used in the software industry as a means through which to price bespoke systems. Under this mantel, construction is the process of building the software solution to a design specification mutually agreed with the customer. The work hour as a charge rate is also common among IT consultants and integrators when supplying design, development or support intellect for customised software.

– Cost-based revenue model: The provider calculates the total cost of software production, adds a markup in terms of required overall profit, and divides by the number of anticipated consumers/subscribers to that particular version of software. If applying this revenue model in the SaaS arena, it is worth noting the going rate for a similar service in the market (Porter 1980) so that the SaaS offering is pitched at an appropriate competitive price. The provider then charges this price to the consumer. Although markup is a core approach in the cost-based revenue model, other examples include cost-plus pricing, target return pricing or margin pricing.

– Data revenue model: High-quality consumer/user data has a value in the CC domain, with the price often dependent on the exclusivity of the information. Some organisations specialise in lead generation, creating and maintaining names and contact information of potential customers before selling them to third parties. For ventures such as Google, Twitter and Facebook, which aggregate high quantities of data about users, the revenue engine is not used as a sales mechanism to sell databases to third parties; these sites focus on targeted advertisements based on customer data mined from their vast databases over time.

Reputational damage can be suffered if such information is distributed or used without the subscriber's knowledge or if subscriber data is criminally breached. Notably, security researchers at the Kromtech Security Research Center have recently discovered a massive database of 560 million login credentials which is believed to come from up to 10 popular online services such as LinkedIn and Dropbox, obtained during previous data breaches (Diachenko 2017).

Under the relational theory of exchange, consumer research suggests that a cohort of subscribers are uncomfortable with online micromarketing, feeling that it equates to 'big brother' tracking their purchases and/or watching their online activities (Achrol and Kotler 2012; Zhang and Krishnamurthi 2004). While this challenge may be less relevant in a B2B environment, SaaS providers should still be conscious of the trust dynamic that needs to exist between provider and subscriber for a relationship to flourish in a CC context.

- Demo ware (or trial ware) revenue model: This demonstration or trial model of the SaaS solution allows users to take a closer look at the system's features before making the decision to subscribe, without being able to use it to generate output.
- Digital product revenue model: Digital goods can be downloaded and consumed instantly. Normally, these goods and services do not have additional production, shipping or inventory costs and there are no major quantity limitations (Laniado 2013), as the download does not need to be 'produced' in the conventional sense. These products include, for example, songs/music from such providers as Spotify or iTunes, eBooks (e.g. Amazon), games and apps (e.g. Google apps) for use on electronic devices such as smartphones, tablets and Kindle readers.

– E-commerce revenue model: This revenue model is the implementation of any of the described revenue models online when in direct interaction with a consumer. The term is less prevalent in the B2B environment.

– Enticement revenue model: This model is sometimes referred to as a 'flash sale'. The approach is built upon a consumer behaviour that motivates an individual to impulse buy (Achrol and Kotler 2012). The approach attempts to entice the consumer to immediately purchase an item based on the tactic that this is a one-off value price that will not be available after a deadline time or date. Daily deals (e.g. Groupon) or flash sales tend to be predominantly evident in the B2C market, although this model has the potential in a B2B market based on annual subscription value offers.

– Fee-for-service or usage revenue model (below): Under this model, the SaaS provider charges customers for the amount of the service they use. This is the closest model to the 5th utility framework outlined in Chap. 3; the more the user uses, the more they pay, much like our approach to electricity supply. For example, a pay-as-you-go mobile phone arrangement is a non-contractual agreement where the customer only pays for the amount of minutes actually used. In the B2B market, measured usage may be based on, for example, pages printed, number of transactions, data consumed or any number of different metrics (Bozkurt 2016).

This is different to the subscription model, which is based on the principles of 'right to use' rather than level of use (e.g. a phone contract, normally for a specified period). The two models are, however, sometimes implemented in tandem in the SaaS sector.

A subset of fee-for-service is the bandwidth revenue model whereby subscribers can gain access to bandwidth on an escalating scale by paying a premium. Entry-level bandwidths tend to be quite low under this model, with incentives built into the pricing strategy to entice users to increase their bandwidth over time. This approach may be particularly valuable if there are significant variations in availability depending on demand (e.g. peak use periods).

- Freemium revenue model and its underlying pricing strategy is discussed in detail later in the book, as it is a popular approach taken by those pursuing initial provider entry into the SaaS market (Bozkurt 2016). In summary, a feature, usage or time-limited version of the software is offered free of charge as an introduction to the system under this model. After the rules of Freemium engagement lapse (time) or are breached (feature/usage levels), the user is prompted to upgrade/register to gain access to a full version of the software. If the user chooses not to upgrade at this point, further use of the system under the Freemium criteria may be restricted depending on the configuration of a particular revenue model.
- Future-use revenue model: Much like the voucher system used by restaurants to allow patrons to buy gift vouchers for meals to be consumed by them or another party at a future date, future-use revenue model facilitates a 'buy now, pay later' strategy. In technology service terms, these revenue options include phone credit, or prepaid credit cards for future online use.
- Licencing revenue model: Sometimes referred to as term licencing (Bozkurt 2016), this is a common model in intellectual property circles, for example, in the use of patents, copyrighted products and services and trademarks. The licence is usually limited by time, territory, types of product, volume (Laniado 2013); hence the use of the word 'term' in its title. A relevant variation of this revenue model in the CC SaaS domain is the provision of certification or trademark software for use in online transactions, for example McAfee SECURE or the Docusign Contract Management system outlined in the glossary of companies at the start of the book.
- Mail order/e-tail revenue model: This revenue model depends on a process where the consumer purchases a product online, which is then delivered by the postal system. This is primarily used in a B2C environment, for example, Amazon goods purchased online and then sent directly to the consumer's home.
- Marketplace revenue model: The Internet creates a unique opportunity to easily connect sellers with consumers, generating new means of revenue generation. The marketplace revenue model assumes a Cloud broker (Fig. 2.4, Chap. 2) exists between the service provider

and end user. For example, Airbnb depends on a Cloud broker to facilitate the hiring of a private owner's room to a visitor through the Airbnb porthole. A platform manager takes care of customer service, payment collection, mediation, and so on; however they do not tend to be involved in providing the service itself (e.g. accommodation) and do not hold inventories. The revenue model is normally based on a specific percentage of the deal (e.g. x% of the total price of the Airbnb room goes to the porthole provider). This revenue model is also used by Apple's iTunes and App store, which take a percentage cut of each sale. Some marketplace coordinators collect from both parties to the transaction; others collect from only one party (which subsidises the other party). Some platform managers (like *Kickstarter*) are entitled to revenues only if the desired deal is fulfilled (Laniado 2013).

— One-time-charge revenue model: The customer can buy a perpetual licence, which allows them to use the licenced software indefinitely (Bozkurt 2016). In addition to the initial licence fee, maintenance, support and updates are usually provided at an additional charge. An advantage of this model is that it amounts to a closed transaction, thus there is nothing for the vendor to keep track of once the sale is made. The revenue is therefore bookable and the customer has his licence. A disadvantage is that if the user requires a software upgrade, the cost can be substantial. There is also little potential to sell on the software if the user no longer has use for it.

— OpenSource: This is not technically a revenue model in its purest form (Niculescu and Wu 2011), as under this model the end user can use publically available, full function, software freely without a licence subscription (Wu and Lin 2001). In its current guise SaaS would position OpenSource as most suitable and appropriate to the Platform as a Service[1] (PaaS) space, and open sourced platforms already exist in forms like Apache and Linux. While OpenSource can have a price tag (e.g. Ruby on Rails and Red Hat), it is argued that these commercial positions come about as an opportunistic market positioning rather than being built into the revenue model from the start. Thus, it is unlikely that the average end user will incur this cost.

- Optioned revenue model: Used traditionally in the international currency market where companies can option a currency rate and agree a price for purchase in the future, this revenue model has gained some traction in the SaaS market. Subscribers can option to purchase SaaS facilities in the future at a defined price for a fee. The option fee is paid regardless of whether the subscriber takes up the additional services.
- Production revenue model: Customised software generation. Under this model, the SaaS provider offers subscribers a service, which they value and are therefore willing to pay for, thereby generating revenue for the company.
- Rental revenue model: Rental enables multiple subscribers to enjoy the same asset at various times. In the SaaS context, the use of the software by a particular B2B subscriber is built on this principle. 'Rent' (e.g. the subscription) can be paid per unit of time, for example, much like you rent a car per day.
- Shareware revenue model: Users are encouraged to make and share copies of a software product, which helps distribute it. Payment may be left entirely up to the goodwill of the customer (referred to as donation ware), or be optional with an online trigger that provides occasional or persistent reminders to register (e.g. nag ware) once the software is in use. The shareware model may have limitations placed on the software version use, for example, that it ceases to operate after a trial period unless the user pays a licence fee. Limitations may also be placed on what software features are available to the user under this model.
- Software licencing revenue model: This licencing revenue model assumes ownership remains with the supplier while right to use is passed to the consumer. For example, the SaaS provider owns a particular content, and retains copyright while selling licences to third parties. A subset of this approach is the software licencing revenue model. Here, software producers sell the right to use their software rather than selling it in unit form. For example, Microsoft sells licences to use their software rather than selling the user a copy of the program. This is sometimes referred to as a 'user licence', intimating limits on the licence, which specifies what the purchaser can and cannot do with the software licence.

– Subscription revenue model: This revenue model has existed for decades, for example, newspaper subscriptions. Sometimes referred to as a fixed-price service, the SaaS provider offers the service to the consumer/subscriber who then pays a predetermined fee for a contracted period of time to use the service. There are likely to be limitations as to the scope and level of usage allowed under the subscription agreement. The subscriber is required to pay the fee until the contract expires, regardless of level or scope of use. If the contract is breached, then there may also be penalties to be paid by the subscriber to the provider. This is a common approach to the purchase of broadband services, download facilities and smartphone contracts in both the B2B and B2C context.

– Usage-based revenue model: This is the fee-for-service model (see above) for the B2B market. The subscriber is charged for the software based on a defined resource usage matrix. For example, pay-per-(multiple)-user or pay-as-you-go. Under this model, usage charging is 'charging for a software product based on some measurable defined metric, often the actual usage during a period' (Kittlaus and Clough 2008, p. 134). The measured usage may be based on amount of storage maintained, numbers of transactions, pages printed or any number of different metrics. According to Kittlaus and Clough (2008) many customers prefer the usage-based model, because many believe that they are light users of some software programs and so it will give them a better price for what is used. It is also a valuable approach for consumers who may only use a particular piece of software intermittently. From the seller's perspective, a usage charging mechanism can make their software available to customers who might not have the financial resources to buy software otherwise, such as small to medium sized enterprises (Seethamraju 2015). Thus, this revenue model allows vendors to expand and diversify their customer base.

This model may be risky for the SaaS provider as incomes may be low or uncertain depending on the take-up by B2B users. Therefore, recouping the software development costs is riskier than with traditional licencing or subscription revenue models. This challenge may be partially alleviated by incorporating a minimum fee for use in a defined period, much like a lower speed limit. On a separate point, since customers do not sign long-term contracts, they can switch to alternatives, a challenge discussed in further detail in Chap. 6. Finally, billing can amount to a significant overhead in the software component industry where this revenue model is popular. With the usage-based approach, it is key for component developers to monitor the use of their software by customers precisely. If the software component is not a SaaS solution, it is very difficult to monitor the usage when the software component is integrated in a secured environment (Bozkurt 2016).

Successful SaaS providers perpetually seek out new ways of generating revenues; thus revenue models continue to evolve in the CC environment. An innovative approach to the creation of an optimised revenue model is particularly useful when applied to new technology and Cloud businesses that are continually exposing new ways to deliver software solutions. The underlying revenue generation approach affiliate to this sector incorporates the various pricing strategies that a SaaS provider might offer to subscribers who want to buy their software solution. Pricing strategies relate to how the subscriber pays for the service, what they pay for, when payment is made, where the money goes and who is involved in each of these subscriber payment options.

4.3 The Art of Pricing

Under a particular revenue model, the pricing strategy amounts to the aspects of pricing related to the agreement between the B2B consumer and the SaaS provider. Despite its significant power in the success of the company, pricing receives scant attention in most companies, with fewer than 5% of the Fortune 500 companies including a full-time function dedicated to pricing (Hinterhuber and Liozu 2012). This neglect is an anomaly considering pricing has a substantial and immediate effect on company profitability.

Of interest in Hinterhuber and Liozu's (2012) research is that pricing power was found to be a learned behaviour. In companies that had achieved higher pricing without a corresponding drop in market share, all had top managers who championed the development of skills in price setting (price orientation) and price getting (price realisation). Regardless of industry, the degree to which managers focused on developing these two capabilities correlated to their companies' success in achieving a better price for their product or service than their competitors. Without this level of managerial engagement, companies were found to typically use historical heuristics, such as cost information, to set prices and yield too much pricing authority to the sales force. Typical examples of cost-based pricing approaches are cost-plus pricing, target return pricing, markup pricing or break-even pricing. These collectively sit under the cost-based revenue model described earlier in the chapter. The main weakness in this approach is that criteria relating to service demand (e.g. willingness to pay, the concept of price elasticity[2]) and competitive price levels when compared to others in the sector are ignored. An alternative route to this pricing strategy is that of customer value-based pricing, a concept explored in greater detail later in this chapter.

Beneath this price mantel, the pricing strategy is the strategy connected to all activities concerning price. We are coming to this topic with the view that innovation in pricing may be a company's most powerful source of competitive advantage (Hinterhuber and Liozu 2014) and yet, in many cases, it is the least explored aspect of an SaaS provider's B2B offering. To comprehend the potential for innovation in this context, it is of value to first explore the pricing strategy options available to SaaS providers currently in the B2B market.

4.4 Alternative SaaS Pricing Strategies in a B2B Setting

Choosing a pricing strategy for software products on a subscription basis is a complex procedure due to the different characteristics of this offering when compared to physical products (Adelstrand and Brostedt 2016). It has become even more complex with the development of SaaS, which has generated new possibilities relating to both payment and delivery of the software. As a result, new pricing models are developed continuously in this market (Bontis and Chung 2000; Harmon et al. 2009) requiring SaaS providers to at least keep up with market offerings. However, reactive pricing strategies are not particularly innovative and are unlikely to provide competitive advantage. By dismantling the principles of software pricing in this market, we hope to enhance the potential for revenue model innovation in this setting.

The first question we might ask in this journey is, how is pricing structured? If we assume cost, customers and competition (Mohr et al. 2010) dictate minimum and maximum pricing bands, then the configuration of a pricing strategy should align to these '3Cs'. Within the software pricing literature, Hinterhuber and Liozu (2012) have developed a pricing capability grid based on two dimensions. The first dimension is price setting, where the provider can set its prices based on cost-, competition- or customer-based pricing while the second dimension relates to how well a provider can realise its prices (e.g. price getting). Combining these dimensions with weak, medium or strong price strategy positions helps us to visualise the dynamics of building a pricing structure in practice (Fig. 4.1).

A weak pricing position can result in (a) providers having no price strategy at all, resulting in sales personnel setting price on a case-by-case basis (labelled 'white flag'), or (b) providers having list prices that reflect customer value but with sales personnel being encouraged to negotiate

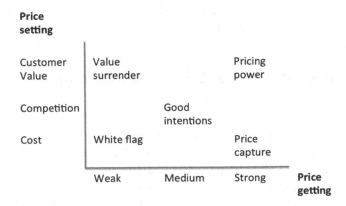

Fig. 4.1 Pricing capability grid (Adapted from: Hinterhuber and Liozu 2012)

heavily without discount guidelines, resulting in value surrender. The medium position is represented by 'good intentions' for those providers working off obsolete pricing strategies. While these strategies had previously maximised value realisation, evolving customer preference has not been taken into account in the interim period, resulting in an out-of-date strategy. Lastly, strong position is represented by price capture when focused on cost to minimise deviation from the list price or pricing power when focused on customer value.

Within these criteria, revenue model and pricing innovation is primarily pursued through a best-value strategy in interaction with customer needs. The application of a power strategy (Fig. 4.1, top right) facilitates value-based pricing, assuming an outside-in perspective (Hunt and Saunders 2013). In addition, customers are segmented based on their service needs rather than through demographics or some other categorisation. The underlying goal in this approach is for the SaaS provider to align their pricing/service strategy with the buyer's value realisation while also making a profit. Thus, this pricing strategy assumes that the needs of both the SaaS provider and the B2B client are taken into account, indicating a more collaborative customer relationship (Bontis and Chung 2000). Those who do not treat SaaS consumers in this way face a higher risk of seeing competitors capture market share and profit at their expense (Achrol and Kotler 2012; Bertini and Gourville 2012).

As discussed above, a provider's business strategy may be facilitated through applying a pricing construct based on those revenue models commonly used in the software industry (see Table 4.1 for an overview). We wish to focus on those in very high use in the SaaS context: Freemium, term licencing/subscription-based fees and the usage-based revenue model. A further option is that of 'one time charge' revenue model (Bozkurt 2016), though this is less likely to be applied in the SaaS context (Table 4.2).

Of interest is that the applied pricing strategies in this market (Table 4.2) do not avail of all of the various revenue models as detailed in Table 4.1, suggesting that there is room for revenue model innovation in this market. Contemplating the pricing strategies outlined in Table 4.2, Freemium as a pricing structure is built on future revenue expectation (Niculescu and Wu 2011). First introduced by the venture capitalist Fred

Table 4.2 SaaS common pricing structures

Revenue model	Description
Freemium	The subscriber is offered access to a basic version of the software or a set trial period for 'free', with the assumption that users will ultimately upgrade to premium use of the full version of the software and/or when the trial period expires
Term licencing/ subscription fee	The subscriber can use the software product over a specific period of time, usually offered at a fixed price often in the form of monthly or annual payments over a contracted period. At the end of this period, the subscriber can choose to (a) renew the contract under existing terms, (b) negotiate a new contract, or (c) abort the contract when the contract period ends
Usage-based revenue model	The subscriber is charged for the software based on a defined resource usage matrix. For example, pay-per-(multiple)-user or pay-as-you-go
One-time charge	The subscriber pays a once-off upfront fee for indefinite use of the licence. This agreement is unlikely to include software upgrades

Adapted from: Kittlaus and Clough 2008, pp. 132–134; Bozkurt 2016, pp. 33–34

Wilson in 2006, it has since become the dominant pricing model amongst Internet start-ups and phone app developers. Its purpose is based on the intent of either eventually moving these early adopters to full fee-paying users or engaging these users as a barrier to entry (Porter 1980) by removing them from the addressable market available to a possible competitor. It is perceived of as the optimum model for providers seeking significant market share in the SaaS market under the assumption that pursuit of market share means the provider needs to reach a large user base.

The term merges the words 'free' and 'premium' and works by initially offering Cloud services for free, while charging a premium for advanced features or adding a charge after a defined period of time. Under this revenue model, the application provider offers the application to its users either as a free service or as one with a lower charge than might be expected to travel with the service level provided. All of this is done with the intention of increasing the numbers of initial users, whether they are paying for the service or not (Clohessy et al. 2016; Niculescu and Wu 2011). The attraction of this strategy is that it allows the service provider to own a certain part of the market but this comes at the cost of having to maintain a costly infrastructure capable of supporting the growing, non-fee-paying customer base which can put the application service provider under significant financial pressure (Murphy 2011) while trying to build their consumer base. This approach is successful when pursuing rapid rollout and accelerated market share growth, but in the long term it does not maximise, or even protect the monetised software product.

Traditionally there have been two Freemium price models that the contemporary information and communications technology (ICT) industry has used: Time Limited Freemium (TLF) and Feature Limited Freemium (FLF), both of which seek to attract the maximum number of end users (Niculescu and Wu 2011). Once introduced, or enticed, to the initial product offering by the 'free' model, the intent is then to convert these free users to 'premium' paying customers, hence the term 'Freemium'. There is an additional pricing strategy, that of Resource Limited Freemium (RLF), which includes a free consumption level after which the user moves to a premium (billable) service, sometimes known as a 'trial period'. Although the pricing model for all three Freemium price models is similar, the free offer for each is different in that in the TLF model, the user is offered the full featured application for free but for a limited time only, after which it would need to be renewed on a fee-paying basis. In a similar vein, but with a different premium catalyst, the FLF model offers the free users a subset of the features of the full application functionality as an enticement or teaser with the full set of features only becoming available on upgrade to the full cost model (Niculescu and Wu 2011). Finally, in the case of RLF, the free service becomes chargeable when a certain consumption limit has been reached (Fig. 4.2).

These pricing strategies are in current widespread use in the commercial SaaS marketplace (e.g. Angry Birds [RLF], Microsoft Office [TLF], and Heroku [RLF]) with Freemium still seen by many as the near-standard market entry strategy for the industry (Murphy 2011). However, not all see this as the panacea for the SaaS industry. Murphy (2011) cautions that Freemium is a high-risk strategy for an industry where the service provision costs continue to grow as the free user base does, irrespective of whether the free to billable conversion efforts are successfully growing at

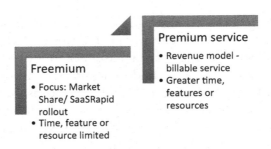

Fig. 4.2 CC SaaS revenue model evolution

the same pace. Niculescu and Wu (2011) confirm this perspective, stating that the cost of maintaining the service while at the same time seeking to convert these users to fee-paying can overwhelm the revenue expectation of a service provider. These authors point to the reality that Freemium is not a strategy with long-term sustainability for commercial providers as it does not embrace the renewal concept. As Murphy (2011) asks,

Why would you need to renew something that is offered for free?

We believe that, as it currently exists, Freemium does not create a compelling CC revenue model, such as would threaten the attraction, or bankability, of true SaaS. For this reason, Freemium revenue models are excluded from the revenue models addressed by this book. The same is true of OpenSource software (Riehle 2009), as it is not technically a revenue model in its purest form.

Beyond the Freemium and OpenSource domain, the SaaS delivery mode depends almost entirely on the pay-per-use or subscription-based pricing model (Fowley and Pahl 2016; Li et al. 2017). This compensation structure is based on ongoing customer usage and revenue generation rather than on the sale of large upfront licences (Dubey and Wagle 2007). In essence, Dubey and Wagle's prediction has come to pass:

As in other radical shifts that have affected the software industry ... players who respond quickly to emerging trends will often be best placed ... Tracking the receptiveness of customers to the service delivery model is critical, so vendors will need to build organisational capabilities to monitor and shape demand. (p. 10)

The usage-based 'pay as you go' model described in Sect. 4.2 offers elasticity and scalability, as well as a high level of virtualisation of Cloud IT resources. Together, these benefits mean the Cloud user can access substantial technological services without suffering the heavy upfront investment affiliate to the development of an in-house solution. Capital investment costs can also be distributed into gradual cost plans, much like the leasing arrangement common in commercial road vehicles. This is part of the reason that CC SaaS is becoming the recommended solution for small to medium sized enterprises (Seethamraju 2015).

Contemplating the most popular B2B SaaS revenue models as discussed above (subscription-based and usage-based revenue models), there are advantages and disadvantages affiliate to each, as summarised in Table 4.3.

Of note is the general lack of research on SaaS involving the subscription revenue model, with the overwhelming majority of SaaS literature focusing on the usage-based 'pay per use' pricing model (Li et al. 2017). This is in spite of evidence from CC providers that they are increasingly reliant on recurring service fees affiliate to SaaS renewal under the subscription revenue model (Clohessy et al. 2016). The biggest capability gap for SaaS providers embracing this new revenue

Table 4.3 Advantages and disadvantages of B2B SaaS revenue models

Revenue model	Advantages	Disadvantages
Subscription-based	Facilitates recurring revenues Diversifies the customer base Increases profit when customers remain loyal Attracts investors, since it causes recurring revenues	Risk of not recouping development costs Relatively low switching costs for customers
Usage-based	Diversifies the customer base Increases profit when customers use the software above average	Risk of not recouping development costs Relatively low switching costs which may facilitate churn Less profit when customers only use the software occasionally/intermittently Monitoring usage metrics effectively can be costly

Adapted from Bozkurt 2016

model and its overriding business model appears to be customer service skills (Dubey and Wagle 2007; Luoma et al. 2012), such that these users are willing to continue to subscribe. Therefore, this book focuses on those revenue models that can facilitate renewal, specifically the subscription model of revenue generation.

4.5   Calculating the Total Cost of SaaS Ownership

While a number of SaaS providers offer an online calculator on their portal to help subscribers estimate the costs of their Cloud resources, this calculation may well fail to address questions of in-house IT resources needed to optimise SaaS use including the cost of maintaining on-premises computers and supporting technology. As such, estimating 'total cost of ownership' of the SaaS solution (Brumec and Vrcek 2013) may be a better calculation tool, so as to include peripheral support costs. This should help the B2B subscriber make a quantified decision regarding the technical sustainability and economic cost effectiveness of purchasing a particular solution, assuming all the security and legal aspects of implementing a CC solution have been considered. It also offers a more accurate comparative tool for assessing other modes of software provision.

As the CC SaaS sector continues to grow, so too do the types of value-based pricing strategies offered to the market. However, these models must also align with the provider and consumer value expectations and realisation to be sustainable (Bontis and Chung 2000). It is these value-based pricing strategies that we focus on next.

4.6   Rethinking B2B SaaS Value-Based Pricing Strategy

As argued above, the lack of costs associated with the physical characteristics of SaaS (e.g. the cost of the medium the software is delivered on) makes it difficult to use traditional cost- or competition-based concepts of margins and markups in order to price this service offering (Bontis and Chung 2000). Despite these facts, Hinterhuber and Liozu (2014) estimate that only 5% of the leading companies in the US, Europe and Asia have embraced the opportunity to evaluate or rethink their pricing strategy, ultimately missing out on a powerful source of competitive advantage. This is due in part to providers looking at pricing on the basis of cost or competition as opposed to customer value. As proposed above, evaluating pricing strategies through a customer value lens can give providers greater opportunities to differentiate themselves from competitors.

Since the introduction of SaaS, provider' cost structures have changed and value-based pricing has become important to justify the gap between the price and the marginal cost for adding a new customer (Baur et al. 2014). This is particularly important in the case of SaaS solutions where the service incorporates hosting and support services, and in the case of complex products that require more service (Buxmann and Lehmann 2009). Thus, when contemplating an appropriate pricing model under the value lens for the SaaS B2B market, the consumer perspective can be expanded to encapsulate the principles of key account management in context. In doing so, SaaS providers can form a particular client's pricing structure based on the value position coupled with the degree of anticipated client interaction with the service (e.g. whether it is unilateral or interactive). In the case of renewals, a subscriber's historic usage and system interaction helps to further refine the offering (Table 4.4).

Once the pricing strategy is formed, it can be further customised based on such criteria as the number of system components used by a client (such as transaction, memory use, concurrent user base, for example) or by applying region- or version-specific criteria. Price bundling can be developed to facilitate heavier users' needs based on an offer, product and integration level or usage criteria. The SaaS provider can also build in a structure of payment flow, such as single payment, recurring licence fee based on frequency and duration of use or some combination. Finally, there is potential to incorporate dynamic pricing dependent on the local market dynamics.

It is worth contemplating innovation in pricing strategy and tactics based on the principles discussed in this chapter. Let us assume that pricing innovation is minimal in organisations that have no pricing team and

Table 4.4 Parameters of software pricing

Price formation	Payment flow	Assessment base	Price discrimination	Bundling	Dynamic pricing
Determination—cost, value, competition	Single payment	No. of components	1st degree	Offer (pure, mixed, unbundled)	Penetration pricing
Degree of interaction	Recurring	Usage dependent	2nd degree	Degree of integration	Post-freemium
Unilateral	Frequency	Transaction	Quantity	Price level	Skimming strategy
Interactive	Duration	Memory	Time		
	Combination	Time	Versioning		
		Other	3rd degree		
		Usage independent	person-related		
		Named user	Region-related		
		Concurrent user	multidimensional		
		Other			

Adapted from: Buxmann and Lehmann 2009

the primary tactic is reactive discounting in pursuit of a cost- or competition-based pricing strategy. This equates to the white flag or value surrender position in Fig. 4.1. Only informed SaaS providers pursue a roadmap for innovation (Hinterhuber and Liozu 2014) that progressively leads to a destination where pricing strategy leverages learning in the provider organisation. When reached, tactics follow customer value criteria and the strategy is underpinned by the principles of participative pricing. Notably, Hunt and Saunders (2013) suggest value-based pricing is not the end game in regard to pricing strategy. They believe that strategy optimisation is only reached when providers have a higher degree of precision around pricing and when decisions are based on refined customer data, built over time. This perspective moves beyond price as the sole basis of performance analysis; thus pricing mastery is built on the principles of continuous improvement in interaction with all indicators and aspects of customer value.

Mastery is assumed when the SaaS provider has integrated business systems and enjoys significant financial returns from rethinking pricing. To pursue this path, providers should first develop a sound pricing strategy on which they can set net prices (Hunt and Saunders 2013). This process includes the development of pricing guidelines and rules that impose the strategy on sales personnel and ensure fairness when dealing with consumers. Those providers who have a strategy and customer net prices in place should consider the process of executing the pricing strategy at a higher level, involving front line personnel. Here, Key Performance Indicators (KPIs) can be developed and managed to connect the underlying strategy to pricing improvements and sustainable margins, as well as a means to evaluate sales personnel (Hunt and Saunders 2013). When contemplating this trajectory, it is important to remember that mastery is not a constant state and that providers can at any stage fall back into the lesser value zones illustrated in Fig. 4.1.

A coherent value-based pricing strategy is dependent on a suitable company culture to be sustained (Hinterhuber and Liozu 2012) as involving the entire organisation in the pricing strategy is far more complex than just changing list prices (Adelstrand and Brostedt 2016). While a full discussion on cultural dynamics is beyond the realms of this book, CEO involvement in and endorsement of the pricing strategy is a vital component in its successful implementation within the provider organisation, particularly if reactive discounting or indeed Freemium has been adopted as a key tactic in the past. A further challenge with this approach is the autonomy of sales personnel when building the customer price. As the adage goes 'old habits die hard' so this discount tactic would need to be carefully monitored as providers move towards pricing mastery, to ensure sales personnel don't revert to old habits.

New pricing approaches often require new organisational structures, capabilities, tools and processes. It also requires different priorities, goals and incentive systems connected to the customer value baseline (Hinterhuber and Liozu 2014). As highlighted in the chapter introduction, the primary driver for a centralised approach to pricing strategy is the attitude and drive of the top management team.

When considering how the internal organisational shift in priorities affiliate to the application of a value-based pricing strategy, it is worth contemplating the criteria that feed into this ethos. Iveroth et al. (2013) propose five pricing model dimensions, each on a continuum. While base (cost, competition, value) has already been discussed above, Iveroth et al. also propose that providers consider scope (package to attribute), client influence (take the price to pay-what-you-want), formula (from fixed price to per unit cost) and temporal rights (perpetual, leasing, rent, subscription or pay per use). Laatikaienen et al. (2013) have since added to this analytical tool by merging it with the parameters of software pricing (Fig. 4.2), adding price discrimination and dynamic pricing strategies to base, scope, influence, formula and temporal rights. They claim that this new model is a suitable tool to analyse companies with products specific to the Cloud services industry. The assumption is that a CC provider can have several subpoints on models of this nature, as its purpose is to help providers capture where they actually are under each dimension, a core ingredient to help map their optimum pricing strategy. Thus, while no formula is foolproof, and all need to be embedded in the organisational culture with a conscious eye on past experience, analytical tools of this nature can help providers pursue a comprehensive and inclusive approach to pricing strategy.

4.7   Moving from Strategy to Price in the SaaS Environment

Having discussed the SaaS market's prevalent revenue models and debated price from a strategy perspective, the question remains, what and how do you charge for the service? In reality, SaaS providers can adopt a number of options, either singularly or in combination to arrive at a price for a particular client based on the preceding analytical frameworks and existing revenue model alternatives (Sect. 4.2) and underpinned by core pricing options (Table 4.1). The final price is therefore calculated based on consumer needs and wants, incorporating one or more of the following:

- Bandwidth
- Bundled options
- By memory use
- By region
- By transaction
- Component or feature-based pricing
- Discount
- Dynamic pricing (local market dynamics)
- Freemium (bound by time, use, other)
- Fee based on advertising
- Integration level
- Introductory offers
- Number of users, concurrent users
- One-time charge
- Pay-per-use
- Pay-as-you-go
- Payment flow: single payment, recurring licence fee based on frequency and duration of use or some combination
- Perpetual licence
- Price list
- Processing power used
- Registration fee
- Special offers

- Storage capacity
- Subscription-based fee
- Timing of usage (peak/ off-peak packages)
- Unbundled pricing
- Usage level
- Version/upgrade

Having the resource in the Cloud ensures that users have licenced access to a shared SaaS resource, without having the cost of maintaining this resource when idle. The key benefits to subscribers are low upfront capital investment, quick rollout and return on investment, minimal in-house hardware requirements, eliminated maintenance costs and updates that can occur without disrupting the organisation (Duhon 2007). However, it is worth noting that SaaS may not necessarily offer cost benefits to organisations that will have the software over several years, as the annual SaaS subscription fee will be higher than the maintenance fees for in-house software.

4.8 The Value a Consumer Places on the Price Paid

Up to this point, we have dissected various revenue models and pricing strategies in pursuit of an optimum price and level of sales to generate sufficient revenue to meet or exceed the firm's financial objectives for a given period. One aspect that has yet to receive attention in this process is the consumer perspective. When a price is paid, the consumer places a value on that transaction (Priem 2007). This can be based on the exchange value which is the price actually paid and which represents revenue to the value system (Bowman and Ambrosini 2000). Many firms assume this is the totality of the consumer value equation (Priem 2007). However, consumers may also place a value on the use they are likely to gain from the purchase. This value assessment amounts to a more subjective evaluation based on the consumer's perceived or actual consumption benefits.

When combined, exchange value and perceived current or future-use value contribute to the total monetary value that a consumer is willing to pay for that service (Bowman and Ambrosini 2000). These views are consistent with the value–price–cost (VPC) framework, where use value (V) is combined with exchange value (P) and C is the production cost of the seller. Here, V minus P amounts to a consumer surplus while P minus C equates to a seller profit (Hoopes et al. 2003). In our experience, there may be a third element to this equation, that of the perceived benefits of dealing with a particular provider. Here, a consumer may place a value on the ease with which the SaaS solution is identified and procured in liaison with the provider's sales and support staff. We have therefore added (E) to the start of Bowman and Ambrosini (2000) equation to represent engagement value in context (EVPC). Let us assume that consumer value capture is the appropriation and retention by the firm of payments made by consumers in expectation of future value from consumption (Priem 2007), based on the adapted EVPC framework. Thus, value is captured when the firm receives the consumer payment, a process that may involve competitive tactics to ensure that consumer does not buy from a competitor.

While much of the exchange value can be dictated by competitor analysis and market expectations (Porter 1980), there is potential for the provider firm to refine the revenue model to facilitate innovation in the engagement and use Engagement Value (EV) criteria. The goal of this approach is to establish or increase the consumer's valuation of the benefits of consumption (use value) or engagement with a particular provider. When value is created, the consumer has a number of options; they may be willing to pay more for a novel benefit or for something perceived to be better. Alternatively, they may choose to receive a previously available benefit at a lower unit cost, which often results in a greater volume purchased (Priem 2007). In addition, they may choose a particular provider based on a positive interaction or series of interactions with that company, on which they place an intrinsic value. Thus, from the consumer's viewpoint, value creation involves increasing use value/engagement value or decreasing exchange value, each of which can increase consumer surplus ([E+V]–P). From the SaaS provider's viewpoint, increasing the consumer benefit experienced is particularly important, as this can result in an opportunity to increase overall revenue received.

4.9   Forecasting the Revenue Stream

As discussed above, one of the most important things an organisation can do for the financial health of a firm is to develop and adopt a coherent revenue model for use in the firm and in interaction with B2B subscribers. However, despite its importance to the very survival of the firm, we have seen that less than 5% of firms have a defined revenue model and/or pricing strategy (Hinterhuber and Liozu 2012, 2014). Furthermore, there is little attention given to the consumer benefit that is derived from expended revenue; thus the individual subscriber appears to be absent from forecasts, appearing instead as a sales aggregate in most revenue stream plans (Priem 2007). This is despite the fact that willing consumers validate the value of SaaS, and, in doing so, have an important role in the forecast process. This discussion looks at both supply (e.g. what the SaaS can offer) and demand (willingness to buy based on perceived value) when forecasting a revenue stream for the company.

The key to creating an optimised revenue model is through accurate supply and demand forecasting, that is, projecting revenue estimates over a specified future period. Certain forecasting models also assume that revenue projections should be matched against the resources available within the firm to ensure the firm is capable of pursuing the projections (Eisenhardt and Martin 2000), a view we adhere to in this book. Resource in this context equates to human resource and the availability of suitable expertise as well as physical resources including software and server capacity. This is an ongoing process that can help the firm to plan estimated income, estimated resource input and how these can propel the firm to meet or exceed its business objectives. There are two such approaches to forecasting: top-down and bottom-up.

With top-down revenue forecasting, you start with the overall market size and use this to identify your market segment (Ehrenberg 2013; Priem 2007). The firm then seeks to identify the segment value in monetary terms to try and predict how much of this market can be captured. This percentage is then used to calculate the total potential revenue. This isn't an accurate process as (a) assumptions are made that market size and value will equate to the estimates for the forecast period without factoring in new entrants or substitute products (Porter 1980), and (b) it assumes that the internal resources and capabilities required to achieve the revenue goals are available within the firm. Under this guise, a capability is the ability to execute a repeatable pattern of actions that creates value for the customer (Osterwalder 2004). The desired capabilities can be difficult to predict without careful consideration of various internal and external factors and drivers and could have a significant impact on the company's estimates if inappropriately forecasted.

Conversely, with bottom-up revenue forecasting, we start by identifying key drivers that will impact revenue generation in a forthcoming specified period. Adapting Lewin's (1951) drivers within his force field analysis theory may of value in context. Relevant drivers include; costs, R&D, customer value expectations, technology, the market environment and the wider economic landscape. There are also a number of internal variables that affect revenue projections in the SaaS market and, when combined with the external perspective, scenario planning (Schwartz 1996) provides a useful basis on which to forecast a revenue stream;

- Define the scope of the revenue forecast (e.g. service level, target market, geographic area, technology delivery). Include a time frame in the scenario, with dependencies such as stage of product and market life cycle, competitor activities and their likely planning horizons. Once this data is gathered, ask what knowledge would be of greatest value to you in deciphering the optimum revenue plan? Look to the past as well as the present when considering your knowledge base—what were the past sources of uncertainty and volatility and will they likely occur in the future? Ideally, employees from various levels and departments within the company should participate in this part of the process.
- Pursue the subscriber perspective. Who will have an interest in the SaaS offering? Who will be affected by any proposed service or price change? Have the key decision makers changed in the prospective client businesses. Have their software needs and expectations altered? How does this differ from the past? Pursuit of a robust B2B client relationship is studied in greater detail in Chap. 5.
- Identify basic trends and key uncertainties facing the SaaS market. What are the relevant political, economic, social, technical, environmental and legal (PESTEL) criteria as they stand today and how will

these PESTEL trigger points differ in the forecast period? What are the unknowns or uncertainties in this regard? At this point it is worth assessing whether specific research is required.

• Check for both consistency and plausibility in the bottom-up trajectory. Shoemaker points to at least three tests here: trend analysis, outcome combinations and likely reaction of major stakeholders. Make a decision that is affiliate to the overriding pricing strategy to ensure consistency.

Adapted from Schoemaker (1995)

These steps incorporate a revenue model approach to attract future clients (Buttell 2009) whilst also seeking to retain the current client base. Scenario planning should also help the SaaS provider to 'draw a broader envelope around the uncertainties and look at them in combination' (Buttell 2009, p. 9), which may alleviate a fear of trying a revenue model that is outside of the normal options. Within the firm, these variables are process specific and depend on what stage the company and the market is in (e.g. start-up, early life, early adopter, growth, mid-life, maturity and decline as simplified indicators of the company and market/sector life cycle). Through this identification process, the organisation is trying to find those variables that have the most impact on their revenue in interaction with their market.

In order to be confident in the revenue forecasts, they need to be seen realistically. There is no sense in hiding from risk; companies should identify it, understand it and directly address it. Companies then need to be able to isolate particular variables so that they can be addressed individually based on these risk criteria (Ehrenberg 2013), in order to ensure that they are contributing to the revenue goals of the company. A sensitivity graph is a great tool for looking at each variable and graphing its potential impact on revenue as it changes. Charting the variable in this way can enable the firm to see at what point revenue improves or worsens based on the proposed revenue model. The goal is to assess the variables and bring them to a point where they can be mitigated (Ehrenberg 2013). Mitigating for variables leads to forecast transparency. Having established the revenue goals and the required inputs to achieve those goals, the company then sets out to calculate the spending required to reach these revenue projections. If the projections require significant additional internal resource, calculations should include both the cost and trajectory of enhancing the sales and support teams and technical capacity as required. From here, the firm can predict how quickly it can scale up based on headcount, technical capacity and milestone projections. Thus, the depth and level of forecast planning requires all departments to be involved to ensure consistent delivery of service when procured by the SaaS provider.

4.10 Selecting a Revenue Model for Your Firm

Once the potential market share and revenue projections are forecast, the company then plans how this revenue can be captured. Based on the foregoing discussion, there are specific guidelines that can help a firm develop an optimised revenue model to meet their organisation's business goals and objectives. This claim is made with the caveat that revenue models are organic in nature. Thus, these models require regular review and refinement, particularly when dealing with an evolving business sector (Porter 1980), as is the case with the CC SaaS market. That being said, SaaS providers should contemplate the following when pursuing an appropriate revenue model in context.

1. Choose a revenue model approach that is best for your company and background. These can be linear or exponential depending on your internal competencies, external opportunities and available resource.
2. The model should allow you to communicate your value to the market and to specify your unique selling points (USPs) to the subscriber base. Without this competency, your organisation is unlikely to survive in an increasing competitive market in the longer term;
3. Forecast the future revenue stream through a resource lens (see Sect. 4.8 above), and be reticent about how far out one can predict with certainty. When contemplating a foreseeable future, a fair guideline is 12–24 months in the CC SaaS sector. Again, be aware that newly acquired resources take time to embed into the organisation, including new recruits and increased Information System (IS) capacity.

4. Contemplate the big picture and take a long-term view when approaching revenue plans. This is an evolving process—the revenue model is not a stationary tool and while the overall architecture of your approach may remain relatively consistent over time, you should continually refine the model and the forecasting approach within.
5. As highlighted above, in the bottom-up forecasting approach, the company needs to identify and assess the variables that affect the revenue forecast. These include internal and external drivers, internal competencies and resource, and external opportunities. Impact should be assessed based on how sensitive the firm is to changes in any of these variables. The goal is to bring these variables to a point where the firm could mitigate them. Adapted from: Ehrenberg 2013

While there is significant choice when it comes to developing a SaaS revenue model and pricing strategy, the key takeaway is that it is vital to have one. It helps the organisation stay focused on its business goals, articulates resource needs when one takes a bottom-up approach to forecasting and provides a necessary foundation for the company's ongoing success.

4.11   Conclusion

This chapter sought to examine the existing software revenue models prevalent in the ICT market and to assess their applicability to CC SaaS provision. The purpose of the presented revenue models is to give the SaaS provider an understanding of its likely cash flow and revenue needs in a particular period. It is also a method through which the SaaS provider can plan how to earn revenue and maximise their profitability based on accurate supply and demand forecasting. In this chapter, pursuit of objective 1 (to examine existing software revenue models and assess their applicability to CC SaaS provision) has exposed interesting anomalies in the current approach to both revenue model construction and pricing strategies within this domain. Of particular interest is the lack of attention given to pricing strategies by SaaS providers, considering the centrality of this strategy to the success and well-being of the organisation.

Furthermore, indifference towards the demand criteria relating to revenue stream generation and in particular comprehending the value a willing consumer places on the service warrants further discussion. Chapter 5 considers the B2B client relationship in the CC SaaS realm in light of these findings, and in pursuit of a sustainable recurring revenue model within this domain.

Notes

1. PaaS is a category of CC that provides a platform and environment to allow developers to build applications and services over the Internet. PaaS is one of three main categories of CC services, alongside Software as a Service (SaaS) and Infrastructure as a Service (IaaS).
2. Price elasticity is the measure of the effect of a price change or a change in the quantity supplied on the demand for that product or service.

References

Achrol, R. S., & Kotler, P. (2012). Frontiers of the marketing paradigm in the third millennium. *Journal of Academic Marketing Science, 40*, 35–52.

Adelstrand, C., & Brostedt, E. (2016). *Creating competitive advantage by rethinking B2B software pricing* (Master of Science Thesis). Industrial Engineering and Management, Sweden.

Baur, A., Genova, A., Buhler, J., & Bick, M. (2014). Customer is king? A framework to shift from cost-to value-based pricing in software as a service: The case of business intelligence software. In *Digital services and information intelligence*, Sanya (AICT, Vol. 445, pp. 1–13).

Bertini, M., & Gourville, J. (2012). Pricing to create shared value. *Harvard Business Review, 90*(6), 96–104.

Bontis, N., & Chung, H. (2000). The evolution of software pricing: From box licences to application service provider models. *Internet Research: Electronic Networking Applications and Policy., 10*(3), 246–255.

Bowman, C., & Ambrosini, V. (2000). Value creation versus value capture: Towards a coherent definition of value in strategy. *British Journal of Management, 11*, 1–15.

Bozkurt, M. (2016). *The price is right? Evaluating revenue models for software component in identity and access management* (Master of Science in Business Administration, unpublished dissertation). University of Twente, the Netherlands.

Brumec, S., & Vrcek, N. (2013). Cost effectiveness of commercial computing Clouds. *Information Systems, 38*, 495–508.

Buttell, A. E. (2009). Scenario planning for your business. *Journal of Financial Planning*, (Nov/Dec), 10–11.

Buxmann, P., & Lehmann, S. (2009, December). Pricing strategies of software vendors. *Business and Information Systems Engineering, 1*, 452–462.

Clohessy, T., Acton, T., Morgan, L., & Conboy, K. (2016). The times they are a-changin for ICT service provision: A Cloud Computing business model perspective. *24th European Conference on Information Systems (ECIS), research paper*, Istanbul.

Diachenko, B. (2017, May 16). Another BIG reason to change your passwords immediately! *MacKeeper Security Research Centre* [Internet]. Available at: https://mackeepersecurity.com/post/mother-of-all-leaks. Accessed June 2017.

Dubey, A., & Wagle, D. (2007, May). Delivering software as a service. *The McKinsey Quarterly*, Web exclusive, 1–24.

Duhon, B. (2007). Software as a service: Why buy when you can rent? *AIIM E-doc, 21*(5), 10.

Ehrenberg, D. (2013). 7 steps to developing your revenue model [Internet]. Available at: https://www.accelo.com/resources/blog/7-steps-to-developing-your-revenue-model/. Accessed Apr 2017.

Eisenhardt, K. M., & Martin, J. A. (2000). Dynamic capabilities: What are they? *Strategic Management Journal, 21*, 1105–1121.

Fowley, F., & Pahl, C. (2016). Cloud migration architecture and pricing – Mapping a licensing business model for software vendors to a SaaS business model. *European Conference on Service-Oriented and Cloud Computing ESOCC – CloudWays' 2016 Workshop*.

George, G., & Bock, A. J. (2011). The business model in practice and its implications for entrepreneurship research. *Entrepreneurship Theory and Practice, 35*(1), 83–111.

Grant, E. (2004). Defining a revenue model for your business. *Business.com* [Internet]. Available at: https://www.business.com/articles/defining-a-revenue-model-for-your-business/. Accessed May 2017.

Harmon, R., Demirkan, H., Hefley, B., & Auseklis, N. (2009). Pricing strategies for information technology services: A value-based approach. *Proceedings of the 42nd Hawaii International Conference on System Sciences*, USA.

Hinterhuber, A., & Liozu, S. (2012). Is it time to rethink your pricing strategy? *MIT Sloan Review, 53*(4), 69.

Hinterhuber, A., & Liozu, S. (2014). Is innovation in pricing your next source of competitive advantage? *Business Horizons, 57*(3), 413–423.

Hoopes, D. G., Madsen, T. L., & Walker, G. (2003). Guest editors' introduction to the special issue: Why is there a re source-based view? Toward a theory of competitive het erogeneity. *Strategic Management Journal, 24*, 889–902.

Hunt, P., & Saunders, J. (2013). *World class pricing.* Indianapolis: Universe Inc..

Iveroth, E., Westelius, A., Petri, C.-J., Olve, N.-J., Cöster, M., & Nilsson, F. (2013). How to differentiate by price: Proposal for a five-dimensional model. *European Management Journal, 31*(2), 109–123.

Kittlaus, H. B., & Clough, P. N. (2008). *Software product management and pricing: Key success factors for software organizations.* Berlin: Springer Science & Business Media.

Laatikainen, G., Ojala, A., & Mazhelis, O. (2013). Cloud services pricing models. In G. Herzwurm & T. Margaria (Eds.), *Software business. From physical products to software services and solutions* (pp. 117–129). Berlin: Springer.

Laniado, E. (2013). Revenue model types: The quick guide [Internet]. Available at: http://www.bmnow.com/revenue-models-quick-guide/. Accessed May 2017.

Lewin, K. (1951). *Field theory in social science.* New York: Harper & Brothers.

Li, S., Cheng, H. K., Duan, Y., & Yang, Y.-C. (2017). A study of enterprise software licensing models. *Journal of Management Information Systems, 34*(1), 177–205.

Luoma, E., Ronkko, M., & Tyrvainen, P. (2012). Current Software-as-a-Service Business Models: Evidence from Finland. In M. A. Cusumano, B. Iyer, & N. Venkatraman (Eds.), *International Conference of Software Business (ICSOB 2012),* (Lecture Notes in Business Information Processing (LNBIP), Vol. 114, pp. 181–194). Berlin/Heidelberg: Springer.

Medjahed, B., Benatallah, B., Bouguettaya, A., Ngu, A. H. H., & Elmagarmid, A. K. (2003). Business-to-business interactions: Issues and enabling technologies. *The VLDB Journal, 12*, 59–85.

Mohr, J., Sengupta, S., & Slater, S. (2010). *Marketing of high-technology products and innovations.* New Jersey: Prentice Hall.

Motley, R. (2004, March). How fast software becomes shelfware. *American Shipper: International Trade and Logistics,* (March), 1–3.

Murphy, L. (2011). Reality of freemium in SaaS. Sixteen ventures [Internet]. Available at: http://pdf.edocr.com/d0406d707a354e842138dfa0383141331 b8edb3e.pdf. Accessed Sept 2016.

Niculescu, M. F., & Wu, D. J. (2011). When should software firms commercialize new products via freemium business models. [Internet] Available at: https://www.misrc.umn.edu/workshops/2011/fall/MariusFlorinNiculescu_2.pdf. Accessed Sep 2016.

Osterwalder, A. (2004). *The business model ontology: A proposition in a design science approach* (Unpublished thesis). Universite de Lausanne.

Osterwalder, A., & Pigneur, Y. (2010). *Business model generation: A handbook for visionaries, game changers, and challengers.* New Jersey: Wiley.

Porter, M. E. (1980). Industry structure and competitive strategy: Keys to profitability. *Financial Analysts Journal, 36*(4), 30–41.

Priem, R. L. (2007). A consumer perspective on value creation. *Academy of Management, 32*(1), 219–235.

Riehle, D. (2009). The commercial open source business model. *Value creation in e-business management* (pp. 18–30). Berlin/Heidelberg: Springer.

Schoemaker, P. J. H. (1995). Scenario planning: A tool for strategic thinking. *Sloan Management Review, 36*(2), 25–40.

Schwartz, P. (1996). *The Art of the long view: Planning for the future in an uncertain world.* New York: Currency Doubleday.

Seethamraju, R. (2015). Adoption of software as a service (SaaS) enterprise resource planning (ERP) systems in small and medium sized enterprises (SMEs). *Information Systems Frontiers, 17*, 475–492.

Wilson, F. (2006). The freemium business model. *A VC Blog,* March 23.

Wu, M.-W., & Lin, Y.-D. (2001). Open source software development: An overview. *Computer, 34*(6), 33–38.

Zhang, J., & Krishnamurthi, L. (2004). Customizing promotions in online stores. *Marketing Science, 23*(4), 561–578.

5

Business-to-Business Client Relationships in the Cloud Computing Software as a Service Realm

5.1 Introduction

In the preceding chapters, we set out the historic background and evolution of Cloud Computing (CC) and chronicled its metamorphosis from earlier forms of technical innovation into its current and more widely accepted role as the software industry's application software distribution platform of choice. As highlighted in Chap. 3, the CC delivery mechanisms are edging ever closer to those of existing utilities, especially where the technical complexity of the service provision and delivery is masked from the expectation of the 'pay as consumed' end user. In this new world, Business-to-Business (B2B) consumer expectation is that Software as a Service (SaaS) will be instantly available when needed in the form expected, much like turning on a light switch, based on a flexible pricing strategy. This revenue model assumes a continuous relationship between subscribers and SaaS providers together with time- or use-dependent metrics (Barqawi et al. 2016), as outlined in Chap. 4.

As this book focuses on the B2B relationship, it is worth contemplating the differences between Business-to-Consumer (B2C) and industrial (B2B) relationships. Very briefly, differences in buying behaviour, the

© The Author(s) 2018
D. Dempsey, F. Kelliher, *Industry Trends in Cloud Computing*,
https://doi.org/10.1007/978-3-319-63994-9_5

evaluation criteria for appraising alternative suppliers, the existence of buying centres are, among others, the most eminent distinctions of industrial buyers. When it comes to B2B services, the context is even more dissimilar because of the fundamental characteristics of services: their intangible nature and the inseparability between production and consumption (Gounaris 2005). The marketing and sales effort and priorities of the B2C and B2B SaaS providers vary accordingly; thus one would be ill advised to apply the principles reflected on in this book to a B2C scenario.

Early CC adopters were likely attracted by the uniqueness of the SaaS offering, which by its nature diminishes as the existing market players or aspirants continue to pitch for a share of the market (Porter 1980). As the SaaS concept is now omnipresent, the more strategic SaaS providers are likely to focus more succinctly on customer relationships as a means through which to secure sustainable revenue streams. With this in mind, it is worth delving into what drives an end user to buy from a SaaS provider. Thus, the focus of this chapter is to consider the catalysts (needs and motivations) of the B2B user to seek out a SaaS solution for their business and to explore these motivations in light of the revenue model that is needed to sustain the SaaS industry (Osterwalder and Pigneur 2010). It also seeks to identify the enablers and barriers that make a subscriber purchase the software service.

5.2   B2B SaaS Supplier–Subscriber Relationships

A relationship describes the kind of link a company establishes between itself and their customer (Osterwalder 2004). As highlighted in Chap. 4, customers have received surprisingly little attention in the business model literature (Priem 2007), despite their central importance to the survival of the company. When modelling the business relationship between a SaaS provider and a B2B subscriber it is important to consider how each party engages with, and in, the relationship.

Customer relationship management (CRM) is a strategy for managing all of a company's relationships and interactions with their customers and potential customers. The Cloud allows providers to build better relationships with customers than has been previously possible in the offline world. By combining the ability to respond directly to customer requests on a virtual platform with the provision of a highly interactive, customised experience, SaaS providers have a greater ability today to establish, nurture and sustain long-term customer relationships than ever before. These online capabilities complement personal interactions provided through salespeople, customer service representatives and call centres. At the same time, companies can choose to exploit the low cost of a virtual customer service to reduce their costs. In order to achieve this level of engagement, companies recognise the need to better understand customer behaviour. Winer (2001) proposes a seven-step progressive CRM framework to help organisations with this process (Fig. 5.1).

To create an electronic database of customer activity is the foundation of any CRM system and is the first step in the CRM framework (Fig. 5.1). This should be a relatively easy task for the SaaS provider, assuming providers record all their subscriber data electronically from when the subscription process begins. As a rule of thumb, data is richer in cases of direct customer interaction and high interaction frequency, as long as this data is captured at the point of interaction (Winer 2001). In cases where data is not captured at subscription and beyond, the database creation would be a far more complex process and is outside the realms of this book.

Fig. 5.1 Progressive customer relationship management framework (Adapted from Winer [2001])

The recommendation is to collect transactions and purchase history with accompanying logistical details such as price paid, delivery date and customer contract details. Depending on the system's features, the seller may also be prompted to capture relevant descriptive information at the point of sale and in cases where further interactions occur early in the relationship. These records could include customer response to marketing stimuli (e.g. whether the client responded to direct or indirect marketing initiatives) and/or a brief record of service calls made and how these were resolved or escalated. The purpose of this data capture from the moment the relationship begins is to build a robust picture of the client success criteria and their experience in interaction with the SaaS provider. In cases where the client makes a complaint or an unanticipated event occurs, an escalation process within this system could trigger a required response on behalf of the SaaS provider. This process is described in further detail later in the chapter.

Once the database is built and the number of clients reaches a pre-defined critical mass, data analysis can begin. The computing process of discovering patterns in large data sets involving methods at the intersection of machine learning, statistics and database systems is titled data mining. There are specific steps in the data mining process, which help with this analysis (Table 5.1).

Traditionally, customer data was analysed with the intent to define market segments. Under this mantel, cluster analysis would help organisations group together clients with similar behavioural patterns, from which they could then build 'target' offerings based on these outcomes. The goal was and is to target the most profitable clients. In recent years, customer data analysis has moved towards individual targets, particularly for high-value customers, as is often the case in the B2B domain.

As the CC SaaS sector primarily depends on renewable subscription for sustainable revenue, SaaS providers have begun to categorise B2B subscribers based on lifetime customer value (LCV). LCV is the current and potential future profitability of a particular client (Winer 2001) calculated based on an extrapolated future revenue model. The goal is to use the customer profitability analysis to separate customers that will provide the most long-term profits from those that are currently

Table 5.1 Data mining steps

Steps	Description
1. Anomaly detection	The identification of unusual data records that might be interesting or data errors that require further investigation
2. Dependency modelling (ARL)	Also known as ARL (association rule modelling), dependency modelling searches for relationships between variables. For example, the SaaS provider might gather data on B2B customer purchasing habits. Using association rule learning, the SaaS provider can determine which services are frequently bought together and use this information for marketing purposes. This is sometimes referred to as market basket analysis
3. Clustering	The task of discovering groups and structures in the data that are in some way similar, without using known structures in the data
4. Classification	Task of generalising known structure to apply to new data. For example, an e-mail program might attempt to classify e-mail as 'legitimate' or 'spam'
5. Regression	Attempts to find a function, which models the data with the least error. For example, estimating the relationships among data or data sets
6. Summarisation	Provides a more compact representation of the data set, including visualisation and report generation

Adapted from Fayyad et al. (1996)

hurting profits or not contributing to them. Identifying high LCV customers in this way provides the opportunity to develop a targeted marketing strategy that may include cross-selling, the development of premium price packages and focused retention strategies, all of which contribute to long-term profit. This analytical approach to customer data also allows the SaaS provider to identify customers that are too costly to serve relative to the revenues being produced. A subscriber exit strategy may be put in place to ensure such revenue draining clients are not renewed.

At this point in the CRM framework (Fig. 5.1), the SaaS provider seeks to build and consolidate relationships with the targeted LCV customers through the development of relationship programs. The purpose of these programs is to both encourage and monitor customer engagement. These programs can include customer service strategies and programs, frequency/loyalty programs, customisation, rewards programs and community-building strategies:

— Customer service strategies and programs: In a general sense, any contact or 'touch points' that a subscriber has with a SaaS provider is a customer service encounter and has the potential either to gain repeat business and help CRM or to have the opposite effect (Winer 2001). Programs can either be reactive (where the subscriber has a problem and contacts the provider's call centre to solve it) or be proactive (where the provider initiates contact to ensure a client is satisfied with the service provided). The proactive strategy sometimes falls under B2B account management, where the team is trained to reach out and anticipate subscriber needs.

— Loyalty/frequency programs: This system provides rewards to clients for repeat purchases (e.g. a discount on renewal). While more common in the B2C market, research confirms that loyalty programs can increase customer switching costs and build barriers to market entry (Cigliano et al. 2000), and are thus a useful strategy to contemplate in the SaaS market, considering the high occurrence of customer churn in this market.

— Customisation: This implies the creation of services for individual customers, which goes against the principles of true CC SaaS provision. However, it could be applied in the SaaS context, based on a charge-per-feature approach. Here, the client is offered a 'choiceboard' (Slywotzky 2000), consisting of a list of features from which they can choose what they need for their particular business. The B2B client customises their service based on this selection process, amounting to a client-specific version. The price is then calculated based on the unit price per feature, in unison with the number of users that will be interacting with the SaaS solution in that client site. This approach is particularly suited to information offerings (Shapiro and Varian 1999) such as those proffered in the SaaS market.

— Community-building strategies: The goal is to build a network of clients who can exchange service-related information and/or to create deeper personal relationships between the subscriber and the SaaS provider. These networks and relationships tend to be referred to as communities or, to give them their full title, communities of practice (Wenger 1998). The goal is to take a prospective relationship with a product or service and turn it into something more personal (Winer 2001). In this way, the SaaS provider can build an environment that makes it more difficult for a subscriber to leave the 'community', resulting in a barrier to switch (Liu et al. 2011).

Customer satisfaction can be viewed either as a process or as an outcome (Turunen 2013). Taking an outcome perspective, the goal in building relationships is to deliver a higher level of customer satisfaction than competing firms deliver (Winer 2001). However, it is worth noting that this relationship does not start as a blank palette. Customers come into the relationship with expectations that need to at least be matched by the SaaS provider's performance. Over time, providers are expected to deliver such performance at higher and higher levels as expectations increase due to competition, marketing communication and changing customer needs and expectations. Therefore, the suggested points of interest for B2B providers when pursuing customer satisfaction include:

– Enhanced communication of technical changes, planned schedules of upgrades and fixes, notice of new products, deals and offers.
– Diverse and customisable options for different sized companies.
– Technical design through a user lens, incorporating ease of use for all experience levels, including first-time users.
– Service quality to incorporate customer support, software launch, upgrades, and retention strategies. Adapted from Turunen 2013

Companies and managers working in sales and business-related positions should also pay more attention to 'rapport' when interacting with current and future customers. Misunderstood expectations and the missed realisation of these expectations can lead to disconfirmation regarding service expectations and quality. Mutual understanding regarding expectations and the realisation of these expectations should be established between the customer and the service provider in order to create higher satisfaction (Turunen 2013).

There is a trade-off between the ability of SaaS providers to deliver a better service based on data access and analysis and the level of privacy offered to individual clients. These privacy challenges should be contemplated throughout the CRM process. The CRM system depends upon a database of customer information and analysis of that data for more effective targeting of marketing communications and relationship-building activities (Winer 2001). These privacy concerns can range from simple irritation if the client receives unwanted solicitation e-mails to a scenario where the client feels their privacy has been violated. An 'opt in' or 'opt out' option can alleviate these concerns. Notably, there are a number of privacy regulations and legislation at the country and community levels that should be adhered to if a provider is to trade in that location and use the CRM tools described in this chapter.

CRM measures of success can incorporate financial and market-based indicators such as profitability, market share and profit margins. They may also include customer-centric measures (Chen and Popovich 2003) such as customer acquisition costs, conversation rates (e.g. tracking an enquiry through to acquisition), retention rates, churn rates, loyalty measure impact and customer share criteria. All of these measures imply the acquisition and extraction of data, ideally with the client's knowledge and agreement in light of the likely privacy preferences as outlined above.

One means through which a more targeted approach to CRM could be pursued in a SaaS setting is by splitting the role of marketing into two parts: one for client acquisition and one for retention (Winer 2001). An alternative split might be that of sales and client relationship management. Regardless of the title adopted, the kind of skills required for each role is quite different. People skilled in acquisition have experience in tactical aspects of marketing such as advertising and sales. In contrast, the skills of retention require a specific understanding of the underpinnings of satisfaction and loyalty for the particular SaaS offering. This individual manages the subscriber's SaaS operation and interacts with other personnel within the provider company whose operations may have an impact on customer satisfaction. An additional aspect of the retention specialist's role is to provide intelligence from market research and the CRM data mining activities.

The focus is on optimisation of the client's experience (Priem 2007) based on the LCV to ensure a sustainable revenue model. In order to pursue this objective, consideration should be given to the SaaS subscriber and supplier needs, motivations and expectations.

5.2.1 Subscriber Needs and Motivation

Motivations for the adoption of a SaaS are varied within and across different sectors, yet there is a value in considering the needs and motivations of the B2B user and to explore these criteria in light of the revenue model that is needed to sustain the SaaS industry (Osterwalder and Pigneur 2010). The SaaS subscriber is a business in the context of this book, although the end user is likely to be an individual. In a B2B subscription, it is generally accepted that the management decision to adopt a CC SaaS system rests with an individual within the business; normally the organisation's top IT executive (Benlian and Hess 2011) or chief information officer (Dubey and Wagle 2007). Therefore, the SaaS solution is often bought or licenced for the end user by the business they are employed by and may then be presented to the end user as a business tool of the company's choice rather than their own. For this reason, it is important that the SaaS provider is aware of who the decision maker is, and is cognisant of the needs and motivations criteria through which that decision maker and their various decision influencers make a decision to purchase the SaaS solution.

A B2B client's needs are built around their system requirements and personal preferences. This needs analysis may include IT cost reductions, operational elasticity, faster upgrade cycles, ease of implementation, required level of performance, level of security, technical complexity, strategic flexibility, access to specialised services, access to information and knowledge, enhanced agility, innovative service delivery and potential quality improvements (Benlian et al. 2011; Garg et al. 2013; Brumec and Vrcek 2013; Benlian and Hess 2011; Clohessy et al. 2016). SaaS technical needs can also include reduced IT infrastructure cost, increased operational flexibility and immediate access to new features and innovations (Armbrust et al. 2010; Barqawi et al. 2016). Needs uncertainty (the uncertainty involved with identifying customer needs) and market uncertainty (the uncertainty involved with matching buyers and sellers) are also included under this mantel.

Coordination costs are those associated with the coordination of producers and customers, including the identification and articulation of needs and solutions, and subsequent optimal matching of buyers and sellers (Berthon et al. 2003). The coordination process includes search costs (finding buyers/sellers), information costs (learning and articulating), bargaining costs (transacting, communicating, negotiating) and decision costs (comparing and deciding). Finally, motivation costs are associated with achieving incentive symmetry and incorporate policing costs such as monitoring activities and performance outcomes and enforcement costs including remedying provider errors (Berthon et al. 2003). This analysis forms the basis for a risk–opportunity assessment as detailed below.

When contemplating control as a motivation factor, Benlian and Hess (2011) found that IT executives 'do not fear losing face or control over resources when weighing the possibility of SaaS adoption' (p. 243), a finding at odds with earlier research (Gewald and Dibbern 2009). The advice given based on these empirical findings is that non-adopters should compare their individual context with those of a meaningful set of SaaS-adopting peers to alleviate concerns in terms of control. A somewhat related topic is the challenges around trust, privacy and personalisation (Dustbar and Wien 2016; Winer 2001), although there has yet to be in-depth research carried out in relation to these criteria.

Likewise, perceived benefits have been shown to influence a B2B subscriber's intention to invest in a SaaS solution, and cost benefits are a primary factor in this regard. Based on empirical research (Benlian and Hess 2011), cost advantages were followed by strategic flexibility in future software selection decisions and quality improvements as perceived benefits of a SaaS acquisition. As SaaS providers support numerous B2B subscribers with a single application code base, deployment time is also reduced and application feature updates are centralised and simplified (Guo 2007). In summary, many B2B subscribers perceive SaaS adoption as a cost-saving lever that can help their business decrease capital expenditure on technology and this can be a sufficient motivation to invest in a SaaS solution. This is not the sole decision point, however, and a best-value rather than low-cost approach may be the optimum strategy for SaaS providers in this market. Of note is that non-adopters appear to overestimate SaaS's total cost of ownership and underestimate strategic and performance issues, as well as specialisation opportunities (Benlian and Hess 2011).

5.2.2 Subscriber Opportunity–Risk Assessment

Prior to contemplating the decision to adopt a CC offering, the subscriber is likely to set out risk: opportunity criteria, through which a SaaS provider can be assessed. The baseline here is that perceived risk is thought of as the felt uncertainty regarding the possible negative consequences of adopting the SaaS solution. This assessment method mirrors the use of cognitive processes based on the subscribers' mental vision of future outcome scenarios (Ajzen and Fishbein 1980); therefore the criteria outlined below are not intended to represent a complete or even comprehensive list. The risk criteria may include performance, assurance, economic risks including return on investment, forecasting, strategic risk, security, technical complexity, customer confidence and managerial risks while the opportunity criteria can encompass cost advantages, strategic flexibility, CC provider core competencies, knowledge transfer, attractive value propositions, access to specialised services, the promise of enhanced agility, innovative service delivery and potential quality improvements (Garg et al. 2013; Brumec and Vrcek 2013; Benlian and Hess 2011; Clohessy et al. 2016). These risks and opportunities are assessed based on the subscriber's needs and motivations as outlined above.

Of the risk criteria specified by potential subscribers, while performance is important, Benlian and Hess (2011) found that data security is paramount. In security terms, examples of vulnerabilities include unauthorised access to management interface, Internet protocol breaches, data access and recovery challenges and metering and billing evasion (Grobauer et al. 2011). Cloud-specific vulnerabilities also encompass virtual machine escape, session riding and hijacking and insecure or obsolete cryptography. At the user level, insecure user behaviour is an ongoing challenge, as users continue to choose weak passwords, seek to reuse passwords and largely apply one-factor authentication mechanisms. Possible risk mitigation strategies might involve developing detailed contracts with the SaaS provider, including security standards relating to data encryption technologies, for example. This contract could also build in breach of service penalties (e.g. if the service is inaccessible due to supplier-caused failures) or data breach occurrences. Safeguards relating to data integrity or outages may also be incorporated.

It is worth bearing in mind that the subscriber and user may not be the same person in a business setting; thus SaaS adoption will ultimately be dictated by the decision maker's overall attitudinal appraisal of the perceived risks and perceived opportunities associated with the SaaS acquisition (Benlian and Hess 2011). Of further note in Benlian and Hess's (2011) study is that opportunities appeared more influential than risks when making SaaS adoption decisions, a view reinforced by Dubey and Wagle (2007) who state that SaaS providers 'must become more responsive to customer needs or risk losing subscription revenues' (p. 4). These findings all point to the reality that most B2B subscribers are unaware of the specialised capabilities that SaaS providers offer (Benlian and Hess 2011). This suggests there is sector-wide potential to move SaaS towards core application areas, which has greater strategic potential for providers as the market SaaS matures.

5.2.3   B2B Supplier–Subscriber Expectations

The above risk–opportunity criteria are not all created 'equal', however, and the decision cycle affiliate to B2B SaaS adoption is a complex process. Performance risks are the possibility that SaaS may not deliver the expected level of service. That is, SaaS does not provide application availability to the level anticipated and/or an adequate network bandwidth to facilitate its optimum use or operation as originally stipulated (Gewald and Dibbern 2009). System outages or connectivity problems can affect all customers at once, generating a high value placed on this risk factor (Kauffman and Sougstad 2008). There are also the risks affiliated to problems of interoperability between SaaS solutions and in-house applications located in the subscriber business. Potential losses due to performance risks can be significant because the day-to-day operations will not be optimally supported if these risks materialise in the subscriber environment. Ultimately, these problems are likely to go beyond an efficiency impact, particularly if the subscriber's own business reputation is damaged due to their customer processes being impacted by a SaaS shortcoming. Thus, the higher the perceived risk, the less likely the SaaS will be adopted by that business.

5.2.4   The Expectation of Value Co-creation

The expectation of B2B subscribers is that value can be co-created with the SaaS provider (Barqawi et al. 2016). The hope is that over time, the provider team will work directly with B2B customers and have a good understanding of their organisational processes and user requirements. To facilitate greater potential for the co-creation of value in this setting, studies have recommended the integration of help desks, case routing and a live chat facility into the B2B subscribers' portal to capture evolving user needs. Sector researchers also point to the benefits of incorporating a customer advisory board into the SaaS management framework and facilitating an early adopter programme in pursuit of emergent needs. By using these kinds of communication platforms, SaaS providers can gain a deeper understanding of subscribers' organisational processes and their use of the SaaS solution. Thus, although not intended as an exhaustive list, the general advice is that SaaS providers should contemplate the following when in pursuit of a value co-creation ethos:

- Clarify respective roles of individuals and teams participating in the service delivery process.
- Concentrate on knowledge sharing with customers, using their direct interactions to actively seek customer feedback and enhance provider understanding of their customers' needs.
- Develop customer engagement platforms to increase the potential to co-create knowledge.

- Encourage a cycle of communication among teams supporting the service so that evolving subscriber needs are communicated to relevant SaaS departments including design and development.
- Introduce technologies to support two-way subscriber–provider interactions to obtain and delivery timely information relating to the service, facilitating early problem and opportunity identification.
- Use of service mapping techniques in an effort to improve SaaS management and service quality.
- Collection of data usage statistics to surface service/adoption issues. Adapted from Barqawi et al. (2016)

This value co-creation potential reveals a need for fine-tuning communications and relationships with B2B subscribers. Specifically, those customer advocates and engineers that support the SaaS delivery process play an indirect but important role in this value co-creation process (Barqawi et al. 2016), as they interact directly with the subscriber business. Appropriately harvested, the SaaS provider can use the information gleaned from subscriber interactions to build new features and functions that may be of value to all subscribers and, in turn, strengthen the value proposition of the SaaS provider. Taking an evolutionary approach to the SaaS solution also offers sustainable competitive advantage to these providers, as market competitors may not have the same access to users. Assuming this approach is sustained, this advantage has the potential to be consolidated as a core business capability in the provider organisation in pursuit of customer loyalty.

5.3   Initial Subscription Criteria in the SaaS Market

The B2B client's initial decision to acquire a CC solution is driven as part of the overall business process, adjudicated on the value of a particular support tool in pursuit of the overriding company strategy. It is assumed that the chosen system 'will be able to predict the demands and behaviours of the hosted services, so that it (can) intelligently undertake decisions related to dynamic scaling or de-scaling of services over federated Cloud infrastructures' (Buyya et al. 2009, p. 5). There is then a divergence in the literature as to whether this decision is made using purely quantitative measures such as technical sustainability and economic and cost effectiveness (Brumec and Vrcek 2013), or encompasses criteria beyond the numerically measurable (Dempsey 2015; Garg et al. 2013).

Research suggests that when first deciding on which provider to do business with, the B2B subscriber contemplates certain non-numeric SaaS provider attributes and criteria before shortlisting or selecting their preferred supplier. Based on a key study (Benlian and Hess 2011) while SaaS adoption intentions are primarily driven by cost/quality improvements, these are considered alongside the level of strategic flexibility offered by readily available CC software options. Further criteria may include performance reputation, contract terms, ease of implementation, predicted improvement in service quality and peer influence.

Once the decision to acquire has been made, service-level negotiations can begin. Negotiations are likely to incorporate both the needs analysis as articulated by the B2B subscriber and the risk criteria identified within this process. Opportunities will be clarified and, where appropriate, incorporated into the service-level agreement (SLA). This agreement is a formal commitment that prevails between a service provider and a client specifying service quality, availability and responsibility of each party in the agreement. This document is also likely to include the cost of service.

Beyond the SaaS market, regulatory requirements and country-specific legislation will need to be adhered to by the supplier. In these instances, awareness of specific language and cultural needs can facilitate a localised offering without restricting the open access benefits affiliated to CC. From a technical perspective, the subscriber's access to a robust computer network is paramount as inadequate network capacity, although outside the supplier's control, can result in perceived low-quality service delivery, negatively affecting the likelihood of contract renewal.

5.3.1   Enablers of and Barriers to Initial SaaS Subscription

While it is futile to try and articulate all possible enablers and barriers affiliated to the initial SaaS subscription, it is worth contemplating those that are common in the B2B context. Here, enablers include the promise of a connected society, a stable technical infrastructure and the digitisation of the economy that has created an open, non-restrictive platform on which to do business. Barriers include data privacy restrictions, restricted Internet access that can often be dictated by national investment in a broadband infrastructure and local or business anti-Cloud policies. Notably, an expectation of losses associated with the SaaS purchase can act as an inhibitor to purchase (Benlian and Hess 2011), regardless of whether this fear of loss is evidenced based.

5.3.2   Impact of Peer Influence

On first subscription, the subscriber may seek out evidence of service delivery quality from other subscribers in the market. Based on this knowledge, the subscriber seeks to measure the cost of service, credit terms, frequency of billing. Thus, perceived value for money as a basis for their decision to purchase a specific CC SaaS package can be influenced by peers in the market. Subscribers may also search for evidence of an existing installed base, reference clients and user case studies in cases where their own industry peers do not have direct experience of the proposed provider.

5.4   Building a Sustainable Client Relationship

An inability to meet or exceed customer expectations is a key reason for client attrition. For a relationship to have an expectation of mutually beneficial outcomes and longevity it must first acknowledge and be built upon the premise of quality support and technical capability (Pring and

Lo 2009). As the subscriber neither owns nor maintains the infrastructure necessary to run the software, consistent service quality may be the differentiator that persuades a B2B client to purchase or stay with a particular provider. To comprehend the subscriber perspective, SaaS vendors should encompass all relevant aspects of service quality management—that is, all cues and events that occur before, during and after the delivery of software services (Benlian et al. 2011).

5.4.1 Delivering Consistent Service Quality and Technical Expertise

Service quality is deemed to be an important factor for both satisfaction and trust in a B2B market (Liu et al. 2011) and the delivery of superior service quality requires an understanding of how B2B consumers perceive and evaluate SaaS-based services. When surveyed, B2B clients identified quality of service criteria as quick reaction times, high technical expertise, evidence of innovations, usability, customer service, regular communications and scheduling of updates, upgrades and software fixes (Turunen 2013). Notably, while this research highlights satisfaction in provider innovations, usability and technical expertise, B2B customers were less enamoured with communications, scheduling and customer service and were also dissatisfied with reaction times. Their key suggestions for enhanced service delivery were improved usability and an easier user interface for first-time buyers. This complexity of perceived service quality is articulated by Micah Solomon when discussing the subjective nuances of customer excellence in context.

> The secret of achieving customer excellence and customer loyalty in my opinion is pretty simple. It's not easy, but it's pretty simple. It's a decision that you make—are you going to put the customer at the centre of your Company, your department, even at the centre of your webforms? Satisfaction follows a predictable pattern. It has three building blocks and a fourth one in case one of the first three go wrong, which unfortunately they will (at times). These steps are; a 'perfect' service, delivered by a caring person, in a timely fashion, with the support of an effective problem resolution process. Take for example, commercial air travel. The only thing that

should matter in air travel is safety. In 2010 there was not a single fatality in commercial air travel in the United States, and there was an article in the paper about that. I assure you, it was nowhere near as big as the article about the flight attendant from Jet Blue who lost it … or as big as one of the thousands of articles about the baggage fees. The safety record was completely dwarfed by all the talk about customer service. You will however be late, you will however be perceived as less than caring and you will have less than a perfect product or service. That is why you need to plan to have upset customers and what to do about it. You need to give that customer a little bit extra. You are not minimising the problem, you're maybe even exaggerating it a little bit. You need employees who will feel invested. (Extract: Micah Solomon, 17 May 2013)

Recent publications have focused on criteria such as security, privacy and trust combined with availability, reliability and resiliency when contemplating SaaS service quality (Moreno-Vozmediano et al. 2013). The assumed baseline is one of consistent, secure, high-quality unbroken service. Notably, SaaS is heavily dependent on the Internet infrastructure, adding a layer of complexity to the expectation of instant availability under the utility perspective (Chap. 3). SaaS offerings have missed customer service availability expectations on occasion and such outages are widely reported (see Exhibit 3.1). As such, service availability is an aspect of the B2B subscriber experience and one that has a direct impact on the client relationship. The amount of flexibility afforded by the SaaS service is of concern to the SaaS subscriber as is the promise of ongoing maintenance/development/ upgrades, and this has a correlation with perceived quality (Benlian et al. 2011). Thus flexibility underpinned by SaaS evolution equates to quality in the consumer's eyes.

Perceived service quality can also be undermined if there is a security breach. This is a shared platform where confidence in the level of system security adopted by providers is balanced with the discomfort of not owning the domain. Customers care deeply if there is a breach in security, regardless if it originated in the provider's organisation. This equates to the analogy of safety in the airline industry being an expected baseline articulated by Micah Solomon above. As such, any security breach reported from the SaaS market will reduce the service quality of all providers in the eyes of the consumer. The same is true of privacy, as it is anticipated that the provider will protect the B2B subscribers' information from exposure. By comprehending the pivot points of service quality (e.g. consistency, availability, flexibility, security and privacy provision), SaaS providers can target investments to improve their service quality and to increase SaaS usage.

Performing client relationship analysis at this higher level allows patterns of strategic concern to be revealed to the SaaS provider. For example, if a provider falls short of B2B client expectation this can be due to a perception that the provider no longer has the abilities to offer a full service, or that the provider does not possess the required facilities or that the provider is not taking on board the client's suggestions (Gournaris 2005). Benlian et al. (2011) propose a measurement instrument for assessing service quality and usefulness perceptions held by SaaS clients, which they call 'SaaS-Qual'. The catalyst to create this tool was driven by the view that firms are moving to more 'high-touch' experiential customer service environments, creating a need to understand the links between customer service design and outcomes related to emotional responses, such as customer satisfaction (Bardhan et al. 2010) in a B2B setting (Gounaris 2005).

Adopting the dimensions perspective of the Service Quality (SERVQUAL) instrument (Parasuraman et al. 1985, 1988) although accepting its limitations in a B2B service setting (Gounaris 2005), the SaaS-Qual factors include rapport, responsiveness, reliability, flexibility, features and security. Responsiveness and security were found to have the strongest impact on customer satisfaction, and perceived system usefulness. Notably, responsiveness and security were found to be far below the minimum acceptable service quality levels among those interviewed. From this picture it is clear to see where SaaS providers should start in an attempt to increase customer satisfaction, perceived usefulness and, indirectly, SaaS continuance intentions. This context-specific service quality measurement tool addresses the distinctive characteristics of SaaS and as such debates the unique service quality expectations of SaaS consumers.

Specific advice includes (Benlian et al. 2011) the negotiation of contractual uptime guarantees or IT helpdesk/ application response times, including penalties and escalation clauses, if the performance standards are not achieved. Granulated SLAs can address specific security needs, including clear data protection and backup policies and regular audits of SLA compliance. By making potentially hidden expectations transparent, the regular tracking of SaaS-Qual results may also be used to (further) inform and specify contractual elements of SLAs such as service-level contents (e.g. targets, time frame), plans for future demand and change management (e.g. joint demand forecasting process), communication procedures (e.g. communication schedules and format), measurement charters (e.g. key performance indicator metrics) and enforcement plans (e.g. penalty/reward definitions). These criteria require complex negotiation processes, depending on the collaborative ethos adopted by B2B suppliers and subscribers, to ensure mutually favourable contractual arrangements.

5.4.2   The Concept of Trust in a B2B Relationship

Research generally differentiates between two types of buyer–supplier relationships: transactional, discrete or arm's-length relationships and collaborative, relational or obligational relationships (Bunduchi 2008). The configuration of the long-term SaaS B2B relationship is more affiliate to the latter and, as such, interdependencies exist between exchange parties in these interorganisational relationships that can either build or impede trust. There are different categories of trust in context; risk-based trust is defined as confidence in one's expectations about another's behaviour, while goodwill trust is understood as confidence in another's goodwill (Bunduchi 2008). Trust can be at a personal level (between two individuals) or at an organisational level. We're assuming that both levels exist in a SaaS B2B environment as the decision maker and ultimate users are individuals as well as acting as representatives of their organisations.

Drawing on social exchange theory, trust builds over time through a series of reciprocal interactions that contribute to commitment and result in satisfaction. Factors impeding trust building in a B2B relationship include poor reputation, lack of effort, difficult/demanding individuals and imbalanced power dynamics (Fleming et al. 2016). In the absence of face-to-face interactions, social exchange may be hampered and the development of personal trust impeded. However, discussion forums and messaging services can go some way towards bridging the human contact gap in a SaaS relationship.

Trust may also be reduced as a consequence of rigid monitoring or control of the exchange. This is true of overreliance on SLAs as a negotiation tool, as an overly inflexible approach can inhibit the building of mutuality between exchange partners. Negative interactions can cause the client to evaluate their satisfaction with the relationship to date, assess their commitment towards the relationship and assess each other's trustworthiness (Tomlinson and Mayer 2009). This process may also result in retrospective assessment of past interactions with the subscriber–provider businesses from a performance perspective (Fleming et al. 2016). This dynamic process of evaluating past B2B interactions involves an assessment of the degree to which the subscriber's performance expectations have been met, as well as the working arrangements between the B2B organisations.

Collaborative activities can support trust building through a number of mechanisms, including the use of feedback, proactive customer care, direct monitoring, communities and the adoption of cooperative norms. Trust can also be enhanced through open sharing of information and through embedding service quality assurance mechanisms in secure technical solutions. This collaborative activity increases the ability for the provider to monitor the B2B relationship, allowing for the early detection of service failure if it occurs. As service failure or underdelivery erodes trust, prompt activity in pursuit of resolution helps to appease the customer's concerns by applying the principles of goodwill trust in context. In some cases, proactive detection and resolution can enhance goodwill trust. Regular communication also enhances provider visibility in this regard. While all of these interactions can occur in a virtual environment, it may be prudent to have interim face-to-face interactions to embed trust at a personal level.

5.4.3 Loyalty as an Evolving Asset in Strong B2B Relationships

While there are various definitions of loyalty, we have taken the view that it refers to the extent to which subscribers feel committed to providers and do not actively seek out replacement SaaS providers (Oliver 1999).

There is no direct empirical evidence of whether a provider's anticipation of what customers' value actually affects customer satisfaction and customer loyalty (Flint et al. 2011) and anecdotal stories suggest that there is no real correlation between these criteria.

> We're all part of loyalty programmes, we think it influences our behaviour in some way, yet very few of us would say it makes us loyal to a brand. Which begs a couple of questions ... the first one being why would we bother as companies having loyalty programmes if they don't seem to generate the thing they promise which is driving loyalty? Even after working in the loyalty industry for the last 20 years, even I struggle with this word 'loyalty'—because it is a very emotive word. Yet very few consumers use the word loyalty ... they'll say I shop here or I prefer this brand. The truth is, in the commercial world when we talk about loyalty, we are actually talking about something that looks like loyalty, which is that customers keep spending money ... Which is a good thing ... but it's not really loyalty, it's repeat purchase and we shouldn't fool ourselves by calling repeat purchase customers, loyal customers. The very best loyalty programs are about ... helping businesses understand their customers.(Lance Walker, TEDxTeAro August 1 2013)

In B2B SaaS relationships, loyalty likely equates to Lance Walker's perspective of evidenced repeat purchase, hence the industry's increasing interest in customer retention and renewal strategies (Woisetschlager et al. 2011). Put simply, customers stay with a service provider because they want to and/or they have to (Liu et al. 2011). In cases where subscribers remain out of choice, empirical evidence suggests that suppliers need to not only be better than their competitors at uncovering and creating what customers value, but they need to also be good at anticipating what those customers will value in the future (Flint et al. 2011). This is particularly necessary in the case of SaaS, as a rapidly evolving market. Loyalty may be a predictor of customer churn (Kim et al. 2004) or a deeply held commitment to rebuy (Oliver and Bearden 1985). In these cases, it can be conceived of as a 'more important customer consideration than even price' (Reichheld and Schefter 2000), as it amounts to 'what I do' versus 'what I feel' (Morgan 2000) in the subscriber's decision approach.

Research has found that relational qualities, including satisfaction and trust, along with switching barriers have significant effects on customer loyalty (Liu et al. 2011). These findings point to the need for strong relationships to be built in a B2B SaaS context, such that both parties can navigate the normal ebbs and flows of that relationship. This is applicable in markets with low switching costs, as is currently the case in the SaaS sector. If we take relationship quality as a higher construct comprising trust, commitment, satisfaction and service quality (Rauyruen and Miller 2007), this helps us comprehend the dimensions of loyalty in context. Notably, Rauyruen and Miller's B2B customer loyalty results show that all four dimensions of relationship quality influence attitudinal loyalty; however, only satisfaction and perceived service quality influence behavioural loyalty (purchase intentions). Thus, while all four dimensions of relationship quality facilitate a sustainable B2B subscriber base, these results point to satisfaction and perceived service quality as key influencers when contemplating the SaaS provider's revenue renewal strategy, in unison with switching barriers within the market (Liu et al. 2011).

5.5   Conclusion

The relationship between the B2B subscriber and the Cloud service provider is one that must be built over time. The subscriber has clearly defined needs and expectations and for the supplier to capture this relationship these needs must be first recognised then delivered against. The expectation of the co-creation of value is a very real one from the subscribers' viewpoint and the supplier needs to pay particular attention to it, so that the value manifests early enough to allow the supplier to position attractively in their potential customer marketplace. The challenge for the supplier is to decide whether the value being sought by the potential SaaS subscriber is as simple as the basic needs of service delivery and security or whether it transcends this to higher motivations. Similarly, the need to reference peer influence is also a supplier consideration. Once acquired the new subscriber must be cultivated and nourished such that loyalty is built towards the supplier by their new-found customer.

References

Ajzen, I., & Fishbein, M. (1980). *Understanding attitudes and predicting social behavior*. Englewood Cliffs: Prentice Hall.

Armbrust, M., Fox, A., Griffith, R., Joseph, A., Katz, R., Konwinski, A., Lee, G., Patterson, D., Rabkin, A., Stoica, I., & Zaharia, M. (2010). A view of Cloud Computing. *Communications of the ACM, 53*(4), 50–58.

Bardhan, I. R., Demirkan, H., Kannan, P. K., Kauffman, R. J., & Sougstad, R. (2010). An interdisciplinary perspective on IT services management and service science. *Journal of Management Information Systems, 26*(4), 13–64.

Barqawi, N., Syed, K., & Mathiassen, L. (2016). Applying service-dominant logic to recurrent release of software: An action research study. *The Journal of Business and Industrial Marketing, 31*(7), 928–940.

Benlian, A., & Hess, T. (2011). Opportunities and risks of software-as-a-service: Findings from a survey of IT executives. *Decision Support Systems, 52*, 232–246.

Benlian, A., Koufaris, M., & Hess, T. (2011). Service quality in software-as-a-service: Developing the SaaS-Qual measure and examining its role in usage continuance. *Journal of Management Information Systems, 28*(3), 85–126.

Berthon, P., Ewing, M., Pitt, L., & Naude, P. (2003). Understanding B2B and the web: The acceleration of coordination and motivation. *Industrial Marketing Management, 32*, 553–561.

Brumec, S., & Vrcek, N. (2013). Cost effectiveness of commercial computing Clouds. *Information Systems, 38*, 495–508.

Bunduchi, R. (2008). Trust, power and transaction costs in B2B exchanges – A socio-economic approach. *Industrial Marketing Management, 37*, 610–622.

Buyya, R., Yeo, C. S., Venugopal, S., Broberg, J., & Brandic, I. (2009). Cloud computing and emerging IT platforms: Vision, hype, and reality for delivering computing as the 5th utility. *Future Generation Computer Systems, 25*(6), 599–616.

Chen, I. J., & Popovich, K. (2003). Understanding customer relationship management (CRM). *Business Process Management Journal, 9*(5), 672–688.

Cigliano, J., Georgiadis, M., Pleasance, D., & Whaley, S. (2000). The price of loyalty. *The McKinsey Quarterly, 4*, 68–77.

Clohessy, T., Acton, T., Morgan, L., & Conboy, K. (2016). The times they are a-changin for ICT service provision: A Cloud computing business model perspective. *24th European Conference on Information Systems (ECIS)* research paper. Istanbul.

Dempsey, D. (2015). *Exploring a business to business recurring revenue framework for the delivery of software as a service through a Cloud Computing channel.* Unpublished Thesis, Waterford Institute of Technology, Ireland.

Dubey, A., & Wagle, D. (2007, May). Delivering software as a service. *The McKinsey Quarterly*, Web exclusive, 1–24.

Dustbar, S., & Wien, T. U. (2016). Cloud Computing. *Computer 49*(2), 12–13.

Fayyad, U., Piatetsky-Shapiro, G., & Smyth, P. (1996, Fall). From data mining to knowledge discovery in databases. *American Association of Artificial Intelligence 17*(3), 37–54.

Fleming, D., Lynch, P., & Kelliher, F. (2016). The process of evaluating business to business relationships facing dissolution. *Industrial Marketing Management, 58,* 83–93.

Flint, D. J., Blocker, C. P., & Boutin, P. J., Jr. (2011). Customer value anticipation, customer satisfaction and loyalty: An empirical examination. *Industrial Marketing Management, 40,* 219–230.

Garg, S. K., Versteeg, S., & Buyya, R. (2013). A framework for ranking of Cloud Computing services. *Future Generation Computer Systems, 29,* 1012–1023.

Gewald, H., & Dibbern, J. (2009). Risks and benefits of business process outsourcing: A study of transaction services in the German banking industry. *Information and Management, 46*(4), 249–257.

Gounaris, S. (2005). Measuring service quality in B2B services: An evaluation of the SERVQUAL scale vis-à-vis the INDSERV scale. *Journal of Services Marketing, 19*(6), 421–435.

Grobauer, B., Walloschek, T., & Stoker, E. (2011, March/April). Understanding Cloud computing vulnerabilities. *IEEE Computer and Reliability Societies,* 50–57.

Guo, J. (2007). Business-to-business electronic market place selection. *Enterprise Information Systems, 1*(4), 383–419.

Kauffman, R. J., & Sougstad, R. (2008). Risk management of contract portfolios in IT services: The profit-at-risk approach. *Journal of Management Information Systems, 25*(1), 17–48.

Kim, M.-K., Park, M.-C., & Jeong, D.-H. (2004). The effects of customer satisfaction and switching barrier on customer loyalty in Korean mobile telecommunication services. *Telecommunications Policy, 28*(2), 145–159.

Liu, C.-T., Guo, Y. M., & Lee, C.-H. (2011). The effects of relationship quality and switching barriers on customer loyalty. *International Journal of Information Management, 31,* 71–79.

Moreno-Vozmediano, R., Montero, R. S., & Llorente, I. M. (2013, July/Augest). Key challenges in Cloud computing, enabling the future Internet of services. *IEEE Internet Computing, 17,* 18–25.

Morgan, R. P. (2000). A consumer-orientated framework of brand equity and loyalty. *International Journal of Market Research, 42*(1), 65–78.

Oliver, R. L. (1999). Whence consumer loyalty? *Journal of Marketing, 63*(4), 33–44.

Oliver, R. L., & Bearden, W. O. (1985). Disconfirmation processes and consumer evaluations in product usage. *Journal of Business Research, 13*(3), 235–246.

Osterwalder, A. (2004). *The business model ontology – A proposition in a design science approach.* Unpublished thesis, Université de Lausanne.

Osterwalder, A., & Pigneur, Y. (2010). *Business model generation: A handbook for visionaries, game changers, and challengers.* Hoboken: Wiley.

Parasuraman, A., Zeithaml, V. A., & Berry, L. L. (1985). A conceptual model of service quality and its implications for future research. *Journal of Marketing, 49*(4), 41–50.

Parasuraman, A., Zeithaml, V. A., & Berry, L. L. (1988). SERVQUAL: A multiple-item scale for measuring consumer perceptions of service quality. *Journal of Retailing, 64*(1), 12–40.

Porter, M. E. (1980). Industry structure and competitive strategy: Keys to profitability. *Financial Analysts Journal, 36*(4), 30–41.

Priem, R. L. (2007). A consumer perspective on value creation. *Academy of Management, 32*(1), 219–235.

Pring, B., & Lo, T. (2009). *Dataquest insight: SaaS adoption trends in the U.S. and U.K.* Stamford: Gartner.

Rauyruen, P., & Miller, K. E. (2007). Relationship quality as a predictor of B2B customer loyalty. *Journal of Business Research, 60,* 21–31.

Reichheld, F., & Schefter, P. (2000). E-loyalty. *Harvard Business Review, 78*(4), 105–113.

Shapiro, C., & Varian, H. R. (1999). *Information rules.* Cambridge, MA: Harvard Business School Press.

Slywotzky, A. J. (2000). The age of the choiceboard. *Harvard Business Review, 78*(1), 40–41.

Solomon, M. (2013, May 17). Customer experience. *Keynote speaker.* [Internet] Available at: https://www.youtube.com/watch?v=lXRJl73KsR0. Accessed May 2017.

Tomlinson, E. C., & Mayer, R. C. (2009). The role of causal attribution dimensions in trust repair. *Academy of Management Review, 34*(1), 85–104.

Turunen, H. (2013). *Customer satisfaction in B2B Cloud services.* Unpublished Master's thesis, Department of Computer Science and Information Systems, University of Jyvaskyla.

Walker, L. (2013, Augest 1). *Customer loyalty programmes... why bother!* TEDxTeAro. [Internet] Available at: https://www.youtube.com/watch?v=5EkiOwoLz-4. Accessed May 2017.

Wenger, E. (1998). *Communities of practice: Learning, meaning and identity.* New York: Cambridge University Press.

Winer, R. S. (2001). A framework for customer relationship management. *California Management Review, 43*(4), 89–105.

Woisetschlager, D. M., Lentz, P., & Evanschitzky, H. (2011). How habits, social ties, and economic switching barriers affect customer loyalty in contractual service settings. *Journal of Business Research, 64,* 800–808.

6

Recurring Revenue Model Through a Cloud Computing Channel

6.1 Introduction

As software services become more ubiquitous, a sustainable subscriber base and its associated revenue are key to the Software as a Service (SaaS) provider's competitive advantage. This shift in emphasis to instant software availability also means that the revenue model supporting the revenue stream of the SaaS delivery is itself becoming more and more dependent on the protection of a continued subscription to the service provided. At the same time, a greater level of end-user choice is emerging in the Cloud Computing (CC) market, as new SaaS providers enter the sector fuelled by the promise of potential earnings. Once this emergent market reaches a point where it is 'fully serviced', early-entry providers are also likely to find it harder to protect their existing client base due to the presence of low switching barriers. Therefore, based on the principles of market dynamics (Porter 1980), competition amongst existing providers is likely to intensify as each provider seeks to do more for less to protect or enhance their market share. In addition, new entrants and substitute offerings are also likely to erode existing provider's market position. As competition heats up, facilitated by the ease of end-user switch-

© The Author(s) 2018
D. Dempsey, F. Kelliher, *Industry Trends in Cloud Computing*,
https://doi.org/10.1007/978-3-319-63994-9_6

ing or propensity to switch (churn), the risk is that providers will be forced to adopt a low-price rather than customer value strategy (Chap. 4), ultimately damaging their potential to make a profit.

As discussed in Chap. 4, there are a myriad of revenue models affiliated to the SaaS sector (see Table 4.1 for an overview). Of these, when one excludes Freemium and OpenSource (see Table 4.2) the most popular models in use are subscription-based revenue streams and fee-per-use models. In this chapter, we will focus on subscription renewal, as the potential for influencing renewal in a fee-per-use structure does not arise. The SaaS subscription model 'composes services dynamically, as needed', thereby allowing the industry to overcome the 'limitations that constrain traditional software use, deployment, and evolution' (Turner et al. 2003, 38). The attractiveness of this differentiation allows the CC service provider to win the initial customer business; however, for sustainable business growth, the act of securing SaaS subscription renewal is equally important for the CC provider. Our particular interest is on 'recurring revenues resulting from on-going payments to either deliver a value proposition to customers or provide post-purchase customer support' (Osterwalder and Pigneur 2010, p. 5). Failure to secure recurring revenue will eventually lead to the business failing or at least requiring continuous subsidy from external sources (Osterwalder and Pigneur 2010), culminating in an unsustainable revenue model. Murphy (2011) highlights this renewal dependency as being unique to the SaaS business, a view reinforced by Luoma et al. (2012). Thus, by concentrating on this aspect of the CC SaaS business in this chapter, we seek to move beyond the customer acquisition phase of SaaS in order to explore the potential for alternative Business-to-Business (B2B) recurring revenue models in the delivery of SaaS through a CC channel. This chapter therefore focuses on the propensity of those B2B customers who are already acquired, continuing to renew their SaaS licence subscription. This boils down to the question:

What Makes a Subscriber Renew?
This chapter extrapolates the findings and outcomes of Chaps. 2, 3, 4 and 5 in the presentation of revenue renewal taxonomy via a CC channel. Component roles include the subscriber (B2B client) and

supplier (SaaS provider in the B2B relationship). The research-identified criteria include service quality, previous performance, reputation, fulfilment of user expectations, contracted terms, peer influence, alternative offerings, external influences, localisation, supplier reputation, trust, loyalty and relationship management. Securing SaaS subscription renewal is critical to the survival and prosperity of the CC SaaS business; therefore any significant attrition, that is, cancellation or reduction of the service, can have a considerable impact on the financial viability of any business based on the renewal model. Failure to renew a subscription is therefore the 'Achilles heel' of CC (McLauchlin 2010).

6.2   Subscription Law of Churn

In light of the accelerated competition levels evident in the SaaS market, the ability to manage churn is key to the survival of the SaaS company, as subscription renewal risk is the fundamental exposure to the successful and continued delivery of SaaS through the CC channel (Fader and Hardie 2007). When contemplating SaaS B2B subscriber attrition or renewal value reduction, it is therefore worth considering churn in context.

The 'churn' rate (sometimes called attrition rate) is the phrase given to the annual percentage rate at which customers stop subscribing to a service (Strømmen-Bakhtiar and Razavi 2011). Dependency on a revenue renewal event and the subsequent risk of churn is not new. This is the same as any other subscription, be it subscriptions at a pay television company (Burez and Van den Poel 2007), insurance premiums in the financial services industry (Peppard 2000), subscription-based telecom (Verhoef 2003) or retail services (Taylor and Hunter 2002). Likewise, the impact of non-renewal is equally devastating to each of these service providers. As McLauchlin (2010) points out that the failure of the renewal will kill the subscription business.

An analogy of churn/non-renewal as a 'leaking bucket' was described in conversation with a SaaS B2B supplier, which may help visualise this activity in practice (Exhibit 6.1).

For visualisation purposes, think of non-renewal as a leaking bucket, where the water it contains is the revenue stream/expectation of the SaaS company. Providers expect the bucket to be continually filled from a flowing tap of new SaaS subscriptions. But the provider is also continually leaking water from a hole, which equates to the attrition, or non-renewal, of previous licensed subscriptions. If the subscription revenue inflow is not greater than, or equal to, the churn or attrition outflow, then the SaaS provider cannot hope to grow or even survive.

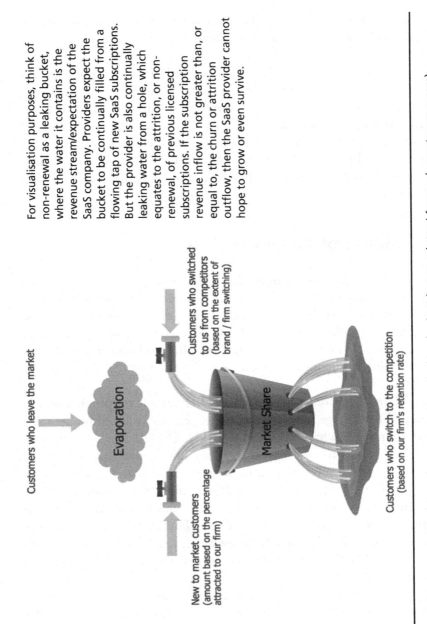

Exhibit 6.1 Analogy of churn/non-renewal as a 'leaking bucket' (Image adapted from: cdn.quotesgram.com)

Based on this analogy (Exhibit 6.1), when the net new revenue flow falls equal to or less than the existing subscription revenue, the business either stagnates or shrinks (Kim and Yoon 2004). We label this activity as the 'Subscription Law of Churn'.

Of note in the highlighted research is that customer churn (propensity to switch providers at renewal), or subscription attrition or reduction, is not a new phenomenon. Renewal motivators are frequently common across subscriptions of all types (e.g. health insurance, telecommunications, media subscription), despite some CC provider' claims that the SaaS renewal model is 'completely different'. The reality is that once the service delivery mechanism is normalised, as is the case by now in the SaaS sector, then traditional and CC subscription renewal criteria have a lot in common. Each has a marketing campaign effort and expense in winning the initial subscription, followed by a business revenue expectation of continued renewal and/or subscription growth. The SaaS providers' sustained success is dependent on the principles of near-full subscription renewal. While the advent of CC brings huge market and revenue expectations (Meeker et al. 2010), it is at risk of failure to (fully) renew a subscription, resulting in either partial reduction or full attrition (McLauchlin 2010). With the SaaS revenue model dependent on renewal, there is a heightened commercial exposure to the failure of the renewal of the subscription licence, with the commercial shelf life of the SaaS application offering not dictated by technological or functional advances as previously in the traditional software industry, but by the success of the SaaS contract renewal negotiations.

6.3 Subscription and Renewal in the SaaS Sector

Without a growing or maintained subscriber base, revenue will drop and competition will grow (Porter 1996), while the cost of maintaining the service infrastructure will need to be spread across an increasingly smaller pool of revenue-contributing customers. Coupled with the fact that the cost of acquiring a new customer is significantly more than that of retaining an existing one (Pfeifer 2005), meeting SaaS user expectations is key to building the recurring revenue model.

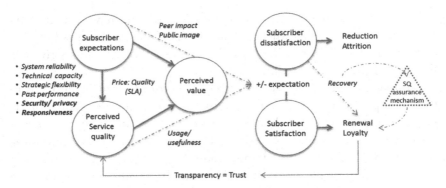

Fig. 6.1 Experience factors framework in the decision to acquire, renew or attrit a SaaS solution (Adapted from the American Customer Satisfaction Index Model (Fornell et al. 1996))

As discussed in Chap. 5, while customer satisfaction can be viewed either as a process or as an outcome (Turunen 2013), we have taken the latter view in our visual representation of B2B customer satisfaction in the SaaS environment. We assume that price and system features are drivers that are likely to be dictated by the competitive market (Porter 1980) and that under a consumer value framework (Priem 2007), the client decision process will also incorporate anticipated experience factors (Fig. 6.1).

Drawing conclusions from the B2B customer relationship debate (Chap. 5), subscription services carry an expectation of trust, service quality and value for money (Burez and Van de Poel 2007), along with a perceived ability of the SaaS provider to perform at the anticipated technical levels. Customer expectations are described as a customer's perceptions of the SaaS solution before initial purchase. Peer impact and the public image of the SaaS provider as reliable are built into this expectation in Fig. 6.1. The customer then forms assumptions around perceived service quality when purchasing the SaaS solution for the first time. These motivators are a combination of user expectation and perception, combined with interpretations of service quality, usage and customer loyalty (Taylor and Hunter 2002). These acquisition influencers incorporate system reliability, technical capacity, service quality, strategic flexibility (including the capacity to customise and innovate), past performance (including reputation, peer influence, known subscriber performance), security and privacy provision, responsiveness and client support. Of these, responsiveness and security are found to be paramount.

Following acquisition, customers equate their SaaS expectations to the service received based on a price: quality equation, often underpinned by their understanding of the service-level agreement (SLA). The alignment of the experienced service quality in light of customer expectation prompts a decision by that customer on the perceived value or usefulness of the acquired solution. Confirmation/disconfirmation of user expectations then occurs (Taylor and Hunter 2002), resulting in the level of satisfaction experienced. Where experience meets or exceeds expectation, customer satisfaction is likely to result in renewal, and sustained customer relationship management (CRM) should build loyalty. Should dissatisfaction occur, that is, that experience does not meet expectation, then the service is unlikely to be renewed at the same level (e.g. service reduction or attrition, depending on the level of switching barriers).

While renewal is the ideal objective, attrition management is also key to the health, success and growth of the Cloud SaaS business (Fan et al. 2009; Luoma et al. 2012). Therefore, there is potential to recover from a negative expectation: experience event through the application of an early detection process, in cases where service quality assurance mechanisms are in place and proactively enacted. Assuming the recovery process is completed in a speedy and transparent manner, sufficient levels of trust in the SaaS provider to continue to provide a quality service following recovery are key motivators to renew the service. Finally, the figure assumes that a feedback loop will add past experience to the next acquisition decision cycle and that over time trust will embed in the supplier–customer relationship, thereby perpetuating the renewal decision process, based on a recurring revenue model bounded by time.

It can be argued that these reasons for renewal are common to all subscription services because these services all carry an expectation of trust, service quality and value for money (Burez and Van den Poel 2007). Renewal criteria are also common across sectors. For example, Verhoef (2003) sets out expectations around service delivery in his paper on customer retention, covering data from market segments as varied as retailing and telecommunications. These are similar to those set out by Peppard (2000) when showing the values expected by a renewing financial services customer.

6.3.1 Customer Value Perspective at Renewal

As discussed in Chap. 4, Sect. 4.8, the value a customer places on the acquisition or renewal of a SaaS solution is based on a combination of value they place on the exchange (P-price), use (V) and engagement with a particular provider (E). This approach to consumer value assumes that each consumption experience adds to the consumer's stock of service-specific experiences (Priem 2007). Thus, the subscriber's decision to acquire, renew or attrit is based on a complex landscape of hard (price) and soft (experience) factors, as exhibited in Fig. 6.1.

In circumstances where the subscriber is contemplating SaaS renewal, the initial subscription criteria outlined in Chaps. 4 and 5 therefore expand to incorporate previous performance on the part of the supplier (Verhoef 2003), fulfilment of user expectations and fulfilment of contracted terms. The subscriber also depends heavily on personal experience of service delivery; and their renewal decision is aligned to the perceived quality of the service provided and the trust they have for the service provider (Burez and Van den Poel 2007). With regard to the supplier–subscriber relationship, trust and loyalty interlock over time, and build through proactive CRM (Chap. 5). Of note is that carefully designed revenue models must be capable of individual subscriber need fulfilment and mutual transparency such that trust is protected and loyalty is given time to mature. Our view of trust, as influenced by Burez and Van den Poel (2007), is one where the relationship between the SaaS provider and their end-user subscriber is one where each party is pursuant of business success coupled with respect and a mutual business partnership.

Of particular importance in the B2B domain is the influence of the renewal decision maker, as this person may not be the ultimate user of the software. As such, they are likely to seek the opinions of the end users when contemplating renewal, creating a distance between the provider, subscriber and end user in this setting. This feedback may have a strong influence on the decision maker's evaluation of the SaaS performance when deciding where to renew, grow, reduce or cease their SaaS subscription. Because of these factors, the SaaS provider should be aware of who the renewal decision maker is, and be cognisant of the specific criteria through which subscribers are likely to renew their subscriptions (Taylor and Hunter 2002).

Collectively, the subscriber–supplier roles in the renewal decision as described above are summarised in Table 6.1.

Based on the foregoing journey from which the B2B SaaS revenue renewal taxonomy evolved, as summarised in Table 6.1, CC is creating a new paradigm for the distribution of computer software applications. Within this context CC-enabled SaaS fundamentally changes the revenue expectations and renewal model for the application software industry, wherein subscription renewal is becoming a primary focus in context.

6.3.2 The Impact of Client Relationship Management on the Renewal Decision

While a non-renewal event is often seen as a stand-alone financial decision or transaction, in reality it sits at the end of a subscription life cycle continuum as exhibited in Fig. 6.1. From the very first connection to the service once initially acquired, the subscriber's depth of usage and dependency on the software is dictated by the perceived service quality in light of the customer's expectations of service levels. Over time, this level of adoption generates a value commitment, which in turns becomes a cornerstone to subscriber loyalty. This loyalty has the added benefit of reputation enhancement for the provider in the B2B market, as satisfied subscribers are likely to be the best form of advertisement through 'word of mouth'.

A breach in anticipated quality, consistency, service and support levels will have a significant impact on the subscriber's belief in the SaaS offering, particularly in the early iterations of service following implementation. If this loyalty is damaged, the likelihood of renewal is significantly reduced, irrespective of cost- or competition- related service criteria such

Table 6.1 B2B SaaS revenue renewal taxonomy via a CC channel

Role	Criteria	Description
Subscriber	Previous performance	Quality of service delivery
	Fulfilment of user expectations	Previous experience, adoption levels
	Contracted terms (SLA)	Achieved levels of trust, perceived service quality and value for money. Cost, credit terms, billing frequency, timing of renewal, perceived customer value
	Peer influence	Market acceptance, existing installed base (dependent on satisfaction levels), user case studies
	Acquisition/renewal influencers	Perceived system reliability, technical capacity, service quality, strategic flexibility (including the capacity to customise and innovate), past performance (including reputation, peer influence, known subscriber performance), security and privacy provision, responsiveness and client support. *Responsiveness and security are paramount.*
Supplier	Alternative offerings	Competitors, new entrants, alternative service offerings
	External influences	Country and community-level security and privacy regulations and legislations, network robustness
	Localisation	Language, business culture fit
	Supplier reputation	Market perception, share of the market
	Trust	Evolving over time is a collaborative customer relationship, perceived co-creation of value
	Loyalty	Initially exhibited through renewal, potential to earn brand commitment over time
	Relationship management	Proactive programmatic adoption of the customer value philosophy, incorporating high levels of service quality and client support
	Recovery management	Early error/fault/dissatisfaction detection process where service quality assurance mechanisms are in place and proactively enacted
	Future proof	Exhibit an innovative approach and strategic flexibility in SaaS provision and solution evolution

as price or software feature richness. This risk may not be visible to the provider at the first subscription renewal, and the subscription may even renew successfully several times, but the reality is that unless there is a full, genuine and early commitment to the SaaS client relationship incorporating a service quality assurance and recovery mechanism, loyalty will not be embedded in the customer relationship. In the absence of loyalty to a specific provider based on experience, renewal is more likely to result in churn tactics on the part of the subscriber.

The decision to renew or cancel a subscription may be influenced by any manner of item or opinion (McLauchlin 2010). Subscription renewal decisions do not happen in a purely objective way as exhibited in the experience factor framework above, but in many cases these decisions can be swayed by interconnected, but often disparate, influences (Burez and Van den Poel 2007), which may not at first be obvious to the service provider. The ability to manage the client relationship in a manner that allows the service provider to facilitate engagement throughout the renewal process has the potential to become a strategic asset for the company over time. SaaS providers who comprehend the different dimensions of the subscriber experience (Sproull 2002) as exhibited in Fig. 6.1 are better equipped to positively influence the renewal process than those who do not have this insight.

In keeping with this perspective, the aim of this book is to help explore the different dimensions of the customer experiences as set out by Sproull (2002). In particular, the concept of objective/subjective influences contributing to the SaaS renewal decision is, in our opinion, an important factor in the consideration of the proposed B2B SaaS revenue model.

6.4 Alternative Revenue Recognition Models and Their Impact on the 'Bottom Line'

In contrast to the SaaS revenue model, the traditional software industry has grown around a classic business model where the typical provider invests heavily in the early stages of the design and build of the software application (see Chap. 4 for further details). Once these 'upfront' investments are made and the software product is ready for sale, the provider then typically seeks to recoup its research and development costs and convert its product into revenue through the repeated distribution and perpetual licence sales of its software solution. In this way, the traditional model depends on the expectation of large, upfront software licence revenues (Brereton et al. 1999; Osterwalder and Yves 2010). Once the classic software company reaches this selling stage it is then in a position to collect and fully recognise the sales revenue received, on payment.

In the SaaS model the revenue recognition of the software licence fee is fundamentally changed. In place of the upfront revenue, the SaaS provider instead will only be able to recognise (collect) the revenue on successful delivery of the SaaS service. The SaaS provider may well license the use of its software application in the same way as the classic software provider, that is, $x per application user or seat; however, in the case of SaaS, instead of the upfront payment expectation of the perpetual use licence, the fee is broken down into a per time period rental, that is, $x per month per user. At first glance this might be thought of as reducing the revenue stream from the software product or service. The reality as illustrated in Fig. 6.2 is very different.

While the monthly rental fee per user licence may be significantly lower that the classic perpetual per user licence fee, nonetheless, over the usage life of the contract, the licence subscription fee will often match or exceed the perpetual fee. As highlighted in Fig. 6.2, once the SaaS application reaches its 'tipping point' (Gladwell 2000), it has a more robust and predictable revenue stream based on the renewal levels, assuming the B2B subscriber stays with the original provider. As Osterwalder and Pigneur (2010) correctly highlight, the one caveat or potential weakness in this simplistic version of the revenue model is that, as presented in its basic form, it is built on the assumption of continued SaaS subscription. We delve more into this topic later but for now it is also worth noting that the total revenue to the software providers is influenced by the software life expectancy and the anticipated customer lifetime value (CLV).

The revenue flow from the two models (traditional software provision and SaaS) is also different. As this simple exhibit shows (Table 6.2), the SaaS marketplace represents a switchover from traditional software sales, with their expectation of significant initial perpetual licences fees followed by predictable ongoing support and maintenance revenue (Fan et al. 2009) to the new CC SaaS business model (Skilton and Director 2010) which sees the revenue stream change to one where the software is licensed and paid for on a subscription basis, as consumed. Over the software lifetime the new business licence sales under both service models may well be the same but Table 6.2 demonstrates how different the flow of the SaaS cumulative revenue streams can be to the SaaS service provider.

Under the traditional model, the bulk of the licence revenue is made available to the software provider in the stages immediately following the finalisation of the initial contracts. A lesser, but still significant, ongoing support and maintenance revenue stream continues to flow and build for the remainder of the application life cycle. The initial payment is front-loaded and recognised immediately on the providers' accounts. This gives the safety of being able to recognise all of the revenue upfront with no financial exposure to the non-deployment of the licences purchased, or 'shelf ware' (Motley 2004). The successful sale of the licence is broadly speaking the successful conclusion of the revenue transaction, paving the way for an opportunity to provide an ongoing and growing

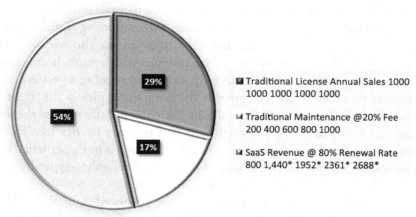

Classic v. Cumulative Revenue $1,000 p.a. Licence Sales

- Traditional License Annual Sales 1000 1000 1000 1000 1000
- Traditional Maintenance @20% Fee 200 400 600 800 1000
- SaaS Revenue @ 80% Renewal Rate 800 1,440* 1952* 2361* 2688*

Fig. 6.2 SaaS licence revenue stream

Table 6.2 SaaS versus traditional licence revenue stream

Year	Traditional licence annual sales	Traditional maintenance @ 20% fee	SaaS annual new licence sales	SaaS revenue @ 80% renewal rate
Year 1	1000	200	1000	800[a]
Year 2	1000	400	1000	1,440[a]
Year 3	1000	600	1000	1952[a]
Year 4	1000	800	1000	2361[a]
Year 5	1000	1000	1000	2688[a]
Cumulative Revenue	5000	3000		9241

[a](Previous year revenue + new sales) × 80% renewal (Adapted from: Fan et al. (2009))

maintenance service by way of an annual fee paid for the lifetime of the software use. Of note is that this illustration shows only the software licence costs and purposely excludes any additional setup, installation and implementation costs. These are often estimated to be higher than the initial licence fee (Fan et al. 2009), but are excluded here for the purpose of normalisation.

The other stream highlighted in Table 6.2 is the revenue flow from the SaaS revenue model. Here it can be seen that the upfront sales revenue is the same as the traditional licence sales figure but it additionally builds to provide a perpetual revenue stream which will continue to grow over the life of the application service, as additional perpetual, revenue flows are licenced and added to the overall revenue stream flowing from the same software application. For normalisation, this stream also excludes any implementation, or additional services revenue, which might accrue from the SaaS application product. In both cases, the number of system user licences provided to the customer is the same but typically the 'right to use' subscription fee will be paid in increments rather than the full upfront payment of a traditional perpetual per user licence fee. This is because in the case of the SaaS, the licence provided is not a perpetual one but instead a right to use for a fixed period of time only—typically on a monthly or annual basis, with the option to renew.

For the SaaS supplier, the initial fee can be enhanced through the addition of an extended term contract. With these fees often collected in advance, this can give the SaaS provider a similar cash flow position to the traditional software provider, but there are anomalies in practice.

While collected in advance, this revenue cannot be placed on the SaaS providers' balance sheet as fully realised until the provider has successfully delivered the service at the user level contracted for the duration of the licence period. Ongoing revenue generation requires continued successful delivery of the service for the contracted period. This monetary realisation approach moves the licence from that of the upfront revenue model of the traditional software industry towards the consumption model of a utility (Buyya et al. 2009). This is the fundamental difference of the pure play CC revenue model, as discussed in detail in Chap. 4.

From the SaaS supplier's perspective, their offering depends on a number of market-led criteria coupled with the relationship they build with existing and potential subscribers (Peppard 2000). Referencing Chap. 4, the price charged is partially dictated by the going rate on the market, particularly when the number of competitors intensifies. The number of alternative offerings will also increase, much like in other utility markets (Buyya et al. 2009), such as the provision of electricity or telephonic services. This perspective firmly positions the Cloud subscription service provider in the revenue expectation arena of any other utility or subscription. Just as any other subscription-based service is subject to churn, so too is the CC industry (Fouquet et al. 2009). This means the SaaS provider, just like the electricity supplier or telephony provider, needs to protect both the need for and its ability to deliver an ongoing service and at the same time closely watch the exposure of customer churn. In the first instance above there is the simple risk of failure to deliver the software service successfully such that it may be consumed as contracted. Second, there is the requirement that the subscription base must be continually protected or grown so as to maintain or expand the overall provider company revenue.

6.5 Conclusion

SaaS as a mechanism for software delivery has fundamentally changed the software industry. The attractions and benefits from this new way of doing business are many and varied, for the service provider and the service user alike. But the SaaS revenue model by its nature is disruptive and its application within the industry is not without its own unique cautions and risks.

For the SaaS subscriber, as set out in Chap. 5, these risks are primarily around the suppliers recognition of, and ability to deliver on, the end users' needs and motivations. When met, the end result is value creation, which manifests as the ongoing trust and loyalty of the subscriber to both the supplier and their product offering. This is an earned trust rather than a single sales outcome and once in place it requires a continued focus for its maintenance.

Already within the industry are examples of the most successful players maintaining a maniacal focus on the business success, which their customers ascribe to the business values derived from the SaaS application services consumed. Once the link between the subscriber success and the supplier service has been built and ingrained, then the subscriber motivation for renewal is established and robust. From this point on, in the eye of the subscriber, the maintenance of this trust is seen as the single most important task for the supplier.

From the supplier lens, the business has invested heavily in the initial acquisition of the customer. Unlike the traditional software revenue model (Osterwalder and Pigneur 2010), the supplier's ability to recoup these acquisition costs from the initial licence sale are diminished in that the revenue stream is not built on the single upfront payments which might previously have been expected. This means that the maintenance and longevity of the supplier/subscriber relationship is now central to both the continued revenue stream of the SaaS supplier and the returns, which they might reasonably expect from their subscriber base. The impact of any churn within this base is amplified for the SaaS provider (Murphy 2011) such that if left unaddressed it could threaten the very viability of the provider business.

References

Brereton, P., Budgen, D., Bennett, K., Munro, M., Layzell, P., McCauley, L., Griffiths, D., & Stannett, C. (1999). The future of software. *Communications of the ACM, 42*(12), 78–84.

Burez, J., & Van den Poel, D. (2007). CRM at a pay-TV company: Using analytical models to reduce customer attrition by targeted marketing for subscription services. *Expert Systems with Applications, 32*(2), 277–288.

Buyya, R., Yeo, C. S., Venugopal, S., Broberg, J., & Brandic, I. (2009). Cloud computing and emerging IT platforms: Vision, hype, and reality for delivering computing as the 5th utility. *Future Generation Computer Systems, 25*(6), 599–616.

Fader, P. S., & Hardie, B. (2007). How to project customer retention. *Journal of Interactive Marketing, 21*(1), 76–90.

Fan, M., Kumar, S., & Whinston, A. B. (2009). Short-term and long-term competition between providers of shrink-wrap software and software as a service. *European Journal of Operational Research, 196*(2), 661–671.

Fornell, C., Johnson, M., Anderson, E., Cha, J., & Bryant, B. (1996). The American customer satisfaction index: Nature, purpose, and findings. *The Journal of Marketing, 60*(4), 7–18.

Fouquet, M., Niedermayer, H., & Carle, G. (2009). Cloud computing for the masses. *Proceedings of the 1st ACM workshop on user-provided networking: Challenges and opportunities*, 31–36.

Gladwell, M. (2000). *The tipping point: How little things can make a big difference*. Boston: Little, Brown and Company.

Kim, H.-S., & Yoon, C.-H. (2004). Determinants of subscriber churn and customer loyalty in the Korean mobile telephony market. *Telecommunications Policy, 28*(9), 751–765.

Luoma, E., Ronkko, M., & Tyrvainen, P. (2012). Current software-as-a-service business models: Evidence from Finland. In M. A. Cusumano, B. Iyer, & N. Venkatraman (Eds.), *ICSOB 2012, LNBIP* (Vol. 114, pp. 181–194).

McLauchlin, J. (2010). Retaining customers: It's not just about the renewal. *The Marketer, 17*(1), 1–3.

Meeker, M., Pitz, B., & Fitzgerald, B. (2010, June). *Internet trends* (Private paper). US: Morgan Stanley Research. [Internet] Available at: http://211.157.29.42/F10Data/HYBG_NEW/DOC/180.pdf. Accessed Aug 2016.

Motley, R. (2004, March). How fast software becomes shelfware. *American Shipper: International Trade and Logistics*.

Murphy, L. (2011). *Reality of freemium in SaaS. Sixteen ventures*. [Internet] Available at: http://pdf.edocr.com/d0406d707a354e842138dfa0383141331 b8edb3e.pdf. Accessed Sept 2016.

Osterwalder, A., & Pigneur, Y. (2010). *Business model generation: A handbook for visionaries, game changers, and challengers*. New Jersey: Wiley.

Osterwalder, A., & Yves, P. (2010). *Business model generation: A handbook for visionaries, game changers, and challengers*. Self published [Internet]. Available at: www.businessmodelgeneration.com. Accessed Jan 2017.

Peppard, J. (2000). Customer relationship management (CRM) in financial services. *European Management Journal, 18*(3), 312–327.

Pfeifer, P. E. (2005). The optimal ratio of acquisition and retention costs. *Journal of Targeting, Measurement and Analysis for Marketing, 13*(2), 179–188.

Porter, M. E. (1980). Industry structure and competitive strategy: Keys to profitability. *Financial Analysts Journal, 36*(4), 30–41.

Porter, M. E. (1996). What is strategy? *Harvard Business Review, 74*(6), 61–78.

Priem, R. L. (2007). A consumer perspective on value creation. *Academy of Management, 32*(1), 219–235.

Skilton, M., & Director, C. (2010). *Building return on investment from cloud computing* (White Paper). US: Cloud Business Artifacts Project, Cloud Computing Work Project, The Open Group.

Sproull, N. (2002). *Handbook of research methods: A guide for practitioners and students in the social sciences.* Maryland: Scarecrow Press.

Strømmen-Bakhhtiar, A., & Razavi, A. R. (2011). Cloud computing business models. *Cloud Computing for Enterprise Architectures*, Springer: London 43-60.

Taylor, S. A., & Hunter, G. L. (2002). The impact of loyalty with e-CRM software and e-services. *International Journal of Service Industry Management, 13*(5), 452–474.

Turner, M., Budgen, D., & Brereton, P. (2003). Turning software into a service. *Computer, 36*(10), 38–44.

Turunen, H. (2013). *Customer satisfaction in B2B cloud services.* Unpublished Master's thesis, Department of Computer Science and Information Systems, University of Jyvaskyla.

Verhoef, P. C. (2003). Understanding the effect of customer relationship management efforts on customer retention and customer share development. *Journal of Marketing, 67*(4), 30–45.

7

B2B Cloud Computing Software as a Service Revenue Model

7.1 Introduction

This book has sought to differentiate Cloud Computing (CC) from previous technical advances and commercial progressions, supported by its own renewal subscription model (Osterwalder and Pigneur 2010). Within this new paradigm, different market strategies exist to secure market share and adoption (Niculescu and Wu 2011). For all their uniqueness in pricing (Chap. 4), customer relationship management and customer acquisition strategy (Chap. 5) each shares a common business exposure to failed renewal subscriptions (Murphy 2011). Here we have taken this business risk as a basis to build a model for revenue renewal to support the CC Software as a Service (SaaS) business. The goal is to identify both the risk factors and the subscription renewal influences such that the debate raised in this text might lead to a robust revenue model for the CC SaaS Business-to-Business (B2B) industry.

As stated previously, the traditional software industry has grown around a revenue model where the typical sector participant invests heavily in its early stages in the design and build of the software application.

© The Author(s) 2018
D. Dempsey, F. Kelliher, *Industry Trends in Cloud Computing*,
https://doi.org/10.1007/978-3-319-63994-9_7

Once the software product is delivered and the production process is ready, the industry player then typically seeks to recoup its development costs and convert its product into revenue through the repeated distribution and perpetual licence sales of its software solution (Cusumano 2008). Once the classic software company reaches this selling stage it is then in a position to recognise the sales revenue received in full, on payment. There are some exceptions to this immediate revenue recognition, such as where part of the payment is held in a suspense, or warranty fund, until final sign-off on the software deliveries by the paying customer. However, although the final licence fee payment may be delayed, all of the revenue still becomes available to the software provider on delivery of the warrantied component. Any delay in payment due to specific warranty agreements does not alter the classical software 'upfront' revenue recognition model.

In the SaaS model (Sääksjärvi et al. 2005) the revenue recognition of the software licence fee is fundamentally changed. In place of the upfront revenue the SaaS provider instead will only be able to realise the revenue (e.g. place it on the balance sheet) once successful delivery of the SaaS service has been achieved (Fader and Hardie 2007).

While the classical revenue model of paying for software upfront is still a core pricing approach in the software market, more and more providers are moving towards the subscription model described above, driven in part by customer rebellion 'against paying a lot of money for standardised or commodity-type software products' (Cusumano 2008, p. 20). The financial markets have responded well to this model, as evidenced by the industry growth predications (Meeker et al. 2010; Morgan Stanley 2011; Sect. 3.4). A Cloud company's deferred revenue is more predictable (Sääksjärvi et al. 2005), and is therefore more favourable from a financial market perspective. This transition to subscription has also generated significant potential to increase revenues for SaaS providers, if they approach their pricing with strategic intent (Chap. 4). Nonetheless, the ability to realise this revenue and therefore document it on the provider's balance sheet is significantly different (Fader and Hardie 2007); thus the purpose of this chapter is to present a revenue model more suited to the provision of SaaS through a CC channel.

7.2 Software as a Service: Contemplating the Revenue Renewal Model

As stated in Chap. 2, we assume that SaaS is a software deployment model through which a CC provider offers applications for B2B consumers to use as a service based on their demand (Lewis 2012). Under this mantel, our focus is on the criteria affiliate to the CC SaaS business model through the eyes of the provider and their consumers, a topic that has been under-represented in the past (Luoma et al. 2012). As such, it is worth contemplating the levels affiliated to the SaaS infrastructure. While Chong and Carraro (2006) suggest four such levels, it is level 4 that is most appropriate under the SaaS mantel. This level is designed as a single version multitenant application and a number of application versions are applied to execute within a load-balanced server farm. This level allows client organisations to consider SaaS as a way to apply business-specific capabilities, which are designed by a third party (the SaaS provider). In doing so, B2B clients do not need to attain, manage and host several software packages or to look for propriety solutions (Strowd and Lewis 2010). Providers of such SaaS services include CloudBees, Engine Yard, Google App Engine, Heroku, Microsoft Windows Azure and Salesforce, among others.

Few publications focus on the opportunities and risks associated with the SaaS adoption decision by key decision makers (Benlian and Hess 2011; Luoma et al. 2012), reinforcing the value of this book as a reference tool for practitioners. Notably, those studies that have been completed have focused on the commercial value of the service within the decision cycle, specifically the price paid. For example, Osterwalder and Pigneur (2010) and Luoma et al. (2012) have each set out some of the many revenue models that are seen as being appropriate for the application software delivery marketplace, and these are included in Chap. 4 of this book. While generally comprehensive, these models tend to focus on the commercial monetisation of the service, excluding or ignoring the option of the model where the application service provider seeks more than revenue from their business proposition, as highlighted in Chaps. 5 and 6. Specifically, while Osterwalder and Pigneur (2010) successfully argue that a robust, protected revenue stream is key to the ongoing commercial success of the provider, it is our opinion that this focus does not adequately address the marketplace where the software provider is not solely motivated by immediate revenue but is equally focused on customer relationship enhancement in pursuit of a sustainable market share.

7.3   Proposing a B2B SaaS Revenue Renewal Model

Having considered the extant research in context, we propose that the decision criteria, which may influence the renewal process, are those set out in the B2B taxonomy presented in Table 6.1 (Chap. 6), repeated here for ease of reference.

Each criterion can have a significant impact on the propensity to renew but the direction of influence for each is most appropriately viewed from the separate and distinct lens of either the subscriber or the supplier. For this reason the criteria have been grouped to reflect both perspectives in Table 6.1. Leveraging from the taxonomy (Table 6.1), we have developed a visual tool to exhibit the experience factors in the decision to acquire, renew or attrit a SaaS solution (Fig. 6.1), again repeated here for ease of reference.

Combining the factors framework and taxonomy, we propose a B2B SaaS revenue renewal model (Fig. 7.1).

The B2B SaaS revenue renewal model (Fig. 7.1) contemplates the supplier–subscriber role in context. There are significant influences weighing on the renewal event. Some are objective and easily quantified (e.g. cost, feature, function); others are subjective and influenced by perception. Equally, some decision criteria move across both perspectives dependent on the paradigm from which they are considered (e.g. adoption, value). Of note is that perception of performance, responsiveness and privacy provision (e.g. service quality) are key determinants of the renewal event in addition to price, feature and function and weigh significantly on the customer's satisfaction level. Level of satisfaction ultimately dictates whether the subscription will be renewed. The model also highlights the

Table 6.1 (replica): B2B SaaS revenue renewal taxonomy via a CC channel

Role	Criteria	Description
Subscriber	Previous performance	Quality of service delivery
	Fulfilment of user expectations	Previous experience, adoption levels
	Contracted terms (SLA)	Achieved levels of trust, perceived service quality and value for money Cost, credit terms, billing frequency, timing of renewal, perceived customer value
	Peer influence	Market acceptance, existing installed base (dependent on satisfaction levels), user case studies
	Acquisition/renewal influencers	Perceived system reliability, technical capacity, service quality, strategic flexibility (including the capacity to customise and innovate), past performance (including reputation, peer influence, known subscriber performance), security and privacy provision, responsiveness and client support
Supplier		*Responsiveness and security are paramount*
	Alternative offerings	Competitors, new entrants, alternative service offerings
	External influences	Country- and community-level security and privacy regulations and legislations, network robustness
	Localisation	Language, business culture fit
	Supplier reputation	Market perception, share of the market
	Trust	Evolving over time is a collaborative customer relationship, perceived co-creation of value
	Loyalty	Initially exhibited through renewal, potential to earn brand commitment over time
	Relationship management	Proactive programmatic adoption of the customer value philosophy, incorporating high levels of service quality and client support
	Recovery management	Early error/fault/dissatisfaction detection process where service quality assurance mechanisms are in place and proactively enacted
	Future proof	Exhibits an innovative approach and strategic flexibility in SaaS provision and solution evolution

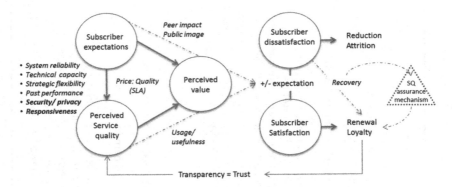

Fig. 6.1 Experience Factors Framework (replica): Experience factors framework in the decision to acquire, renew or attrit a SaaS solution (Adapted from the American Customer Satisfaction Index Model (Fornell et al. [1996]))

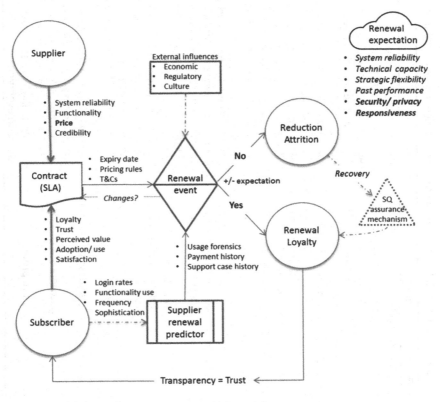

Fig. 7.1 Initial B2B SaaS revenue renewal model

independent/dependent elements of the renewal event. Each has a weighting, which differs in influence for each unique renewal event. It is this influence and its impact on the subscription renewal which poses the business risk for the SaaS supplier.

McLauchlin (2010) sets out the dependency of the SaaS business on the successful renewal of the previous contract; yet how can the supplier predict the outcome with so many external subjective influences capable of impacting its outcome? When considering the revenue renewal model we included the criteria supported by prior research, presented in the taxonomy (Table 6.1) and experience factors framework (Fig. 6.1) as well as our professional insight:

a) A key tenant of a subscription is that one is never the owner of the software but rather has the right to access, use or reference the knowledge it contains. It also implies that this service access is time bound which means that ongoing, updated access to the subscription or service has to be renewed periodically if the B2B user is to continue to have an updated and maintained service level.

b) The fundamental difference between a CC subscription and any other service or subscription is that the knowledge or value-added data created or owned by the user no longer rests with them on a failed renewal. This remote placement of the data adds an extra dimension to the SaaS renewal decision and could therefore also be considered as an additional variable not present in the analysis of more traditional subscriptions.

c) In developing a model of SaaS revenue renewal, it is important to also consider the timing of the renewal, in particular what data should be extrapolated relating to the renewal? Key questions relating to this dilemma include should the data analysis be based on a snapshot of the subscription renewal data at a particular point in time? Or, should it be based on a particular cycle in the business or a point in time in the calendar of the user? These are important considerations, which could easily influence the renewal outcome.

d) The revenue renewal model should consider the democratisation of software use, which is positioned as one of the strengths of 'true' CC. One of the tenets of CC is that one product is offered across many user segments, ranging from the smallest single user to the multinational business with many thousands of users (Marston et al. 2011). The functionality offered may vary across editions of the subscription product but the fundamental question of a subscription expiry and renewal is applicable to all. However, the renewal decision in one segment will have fundamentally different objective and subjective judgements from the renewal decision in another. Therefore the model focus is on the B2B user cohort only.

e) There is also the question of the location of the subscription user. This brings many influences on the usage and adoption of the product set, all of which will impact on the likelihood of the SaaS being renewed. The attractiveness of a software offering and its subsequent renewal propensity are very different in its home and remote markets.

f) While one could undertake data analysis with the sole intent to measure something as straightforward as a series of reasons for not renewing, the reality is that each of these reasons is a single-dimensional view of the data and stand-alone and provides little meaningful insight into the subscription renewal decision process as exhibited in Fig. 6.1. For this reason a more subjective approach is called for through which the decision process itself is considered.

7.4 Conclusion

The revenue model set out in this chapter is one driven by the perceived value derived by the business subscriber from the SaaS application. This value manifests as either a customer experience, which sets the expectation levels that the subscriber brings into their renewal cycle, or a supplier experience, which quantifies the value and returns from the efforts required to meet the customer needs. Whether either experience is perceived of as positive or negative is of key importance both to the supplier and to the subscriber alike in that the performance of either will shape their respective views of their ongoing relationship.

The transient nature of SaaS service means that the product value itself only exists if the relationship is maintained and healthy. Anything less and the business value can quickly disappear for both parties. This means that the revenue model for the industry must be built around a fundamental expectation of an ongoing subscription stream, underpinned by the earned trust of the service subscriber. The revenue model proposed in this chapter sets out the inputs and inflectional points of such a business model and, in particular, identifies any external influences which might, mutually or stand-alone, impact the viability of the SaaS supplier–subscriber commercial relationship.

References

Benlian, A., & Hess, T. (2011). Opportunities and risks of software-as-a-service: Findings from a survey of IT executives. *Decision Support Systems, 52*, 232–246.

Chong, F., & Carraro, G. (2006). *Architecture strategies for catching the long tail.* [Internet] Available at: www.msdn.microsoft.com/en-us/library/aa479069. aspx. Accessed Nov 2016.

Cusumano, M. (2008). The changing software business: Moving from products to services. *Computer, 41*(1), 20–27.

Fader, P. S., & Hardie, B. (2007). How to project customer retention. *Journal of Interactive Marketing, 21*(1), 76–90.

Fornell, C., Johnson, M., Anderson, E., Cha, J., & Bryant, B. (1996). The American customer satisfaction index: Nature, purpose, and findings. *The Journal of Marketing, 60*(4), 7–18.

Lewis, G. A. (2012). *The role of standards in Cloud-computing interoperability.* US: Software Engineering Institute, Carnegie Mellon University.

Luoma, E., Ronkko, M., & Tyrvainen, P. (2012). Current software-as-a-service business models: Evidence from Finland. In M. A. Cusumano, B. Iyer, & N. Venkatraman (Eds.), In *International Conference of Software Business (ICSOB 2012)*, (Lecture Notes in Business Information Processing (LNBIP), Vol. 114, pp. 181–194). Berlin/Heidelberg: Springer.

Marston, S., Li, Z., Bandyopadhyay, S., Zhang, J., & Ghalsasi, A. (2011). Cloud computing – The business perspective. *Decision Support Systems, 51*(1), 176–189.

McLauchlin, J. (2010). Retaining customers: It's not just about the renewal. *The Marketer, 17*(1), 1–3.

Meeker, M., Pitz, B., & Fitzgerald, B. (2010, June). *Internet trends*. US: Morgan Stanley Research. Private Paper. [Internet] Available at: http://211.157.29.42/F10Data/HYBG_NEW/DOC/180.pdf. Accessed Aug 2016.

Morgan Stanley. (2011, May 23). *Cloud computing takes off: Market set to boom as migration accelerates.* Morgan Stanley Blue Paper. [Internet] Available at: http://www.morganstanley.com/views/perspectives/Cloud_computing.pdf. Accessed Aug 2016.

Murphy, L. (2011). *Reality of freemium in SaaS.* Sixteen Ventures. [Internet] Available at: http://pdf.edocr.com/d0406d707a354e842138dfa0383141331 b8edb3e.pdf. Accessed Sept 2016.

Niculescu, M. F., & Wu, D. J. (2011). When should software firms commercialize new products via freemium business models. *Under Review.* [Internet] Available at: https://www.misrc.umn.edu/workshops/2011/fall/MariusFlorin Niculescu_2.pdf. Accessed Sept 2016.

Osterwalder, A., & Pigneur, Y. (2010). *Business model generation: A handbook for visionaries, game changers, and challengers.* Hoboken: Wiley.

Sääksjärvi, M., Lassila, A., & Nordstrom, H. (2005). Evaluating the software as a service business model: From CPU time-sharing to online innovation sharing. *IADIS International Conference e-Society.*

Strowd, H. D., & Lewis, G. A. (2010). *T-Check in system-of-systems technologies: Cloud computing.* US: Software Engineering Institute, Carnegie Mellon University.

8

Recurring Revenue Model in Practice

8.1 Introduction

In their classic guise, the traditional revenue models have served the software industry well. But now, with Cloud Computing (CC) established as the new industry standard for the delivery of application software, this model is outdated and is fast becoming less and less appropriate. The pitfalls and exposures of the old model—shelf-ware, version control, operating system variations, and language and currency conversions—have largely disappeared with the delivery of software applications through the CC channel. However, the new delivery methodology also brings fresh challenges of its own—most notably that of the exposure of the industry to the non-renewal of the recurring subscription revenue or attrition to another provider due to churn. The history and the theoretical side of these churn risks have been set out in Chap. 6 but what do these risks look like in the real world? Following conceptualisation of the proposed revenue renewal model (Fig. 7.1), we sought to study this model's application in practice and to update Fig. 7.1 based on the outcomes of the primary research documented in this chapter.

© The Author(s) 2018
D. Dempsey, F. Kelliher, *Industry Trends in Cloud Computing*,
https://doi.org/10.1007/978-3-319-63994-9_8

When beginning the research process we first took a deep breath, stood back and looked at what exactly it was that we were proposing to research and why. Was it to measure the statistical performance of the renewal events or was it to understand why these renewal events happened in the first place? In other words, which influenced which? This decision wasn't as easy a resolution for us as it might first seem. The tracking and measurement of each of these factors was considered important and relevant as indicators of the likely success or otherwise of the CC Software as a Service (SaaS) business and we vacillated from one to the other in terms of which carried the most weight to begin with. Surely the numbers were the most important indicator? But then, equally, what about the experience factors exhibited in Fig. 6.1? Without understanding these factors alongside the criteria identified in the research-informed taxonomy (Table 6.1), how could we hope to predict the outcome of the renewal event? It was a classic chicken and egg situation and our causality dilemma sat squarely in the middle. Our moment of clarity finally came when we realised that it was neither one nor the other but both.

The reality is that this investigation was not simply about value creation or even co-creation with the supplier and subscriber as equal parties in a business relationship, but also about value perception and value maintenance. Thus, to truly surface renewal performance indicators in the proposed revenue renewal model, we needed to carefully consider the key aspects of what was occurring—the who, what, when, where, how and why of the attrition or renewal decision.

Focused on the core tenet of the research study, we sought to measure and analyse real-life attrition data to comprehend what had happened and why? In order to build a meaningful and complete analysis and interpretation of the research findings we needed both the hard, objective attrition performance data of the actual attrition event coupled with the softer, more subjective data points which might have influenced these attritions. We needed to go beyond the simple categorisation of a series of reason codes (Linstone 1985), as merely relating these coded decisions to a quantifiable number based on the analysis of previous performance would still leave us with a single-dimensional view of the data. Of itself, this would provide little meaningful insight into the renewal decision. To truly understand the subscription decision process, we strongly believed that we would need to also gain an understanding of the subscriber's subjective reasoning at the time when the subscriber was making the decision to renew or not. This meant that we would need to not alone look at the statistical renewal performance but we would also need to probe deeper into the drivers, influences and experience factors shaping that commercial decision.

With these underpinnings now clear, and supported by our conceptual model, we gave our undivided attention to identifying the appropriate cohort through which to study the proposed Business-to-Business (B2B) revenue renewal model in practice.

8.2 Analysing Customer Relationship Data

To support this industry research we approached a leading Cloud service provider for assistance in accessing real-world attrition data. Typical of the industry leadership position earned by this company, we were graciously supported in our request. The service provider in question had maintained a laser commercial focus on the renewal of its B2B subscriptions and, in doing so it continuously elicited and tracked the views of its renewing and attriting B2B customers.

We were given access to a data set containing over 10,000 B2B SaaS customer renewal/attrition historic exit data records. These records listed both full and partial attritions, coupled with the historic renewal exit reasons cited. Anonymised to remove any individual or commercially sensitive detail, this data was consolidated and used as a basis for the analysis of any patterns or trends that might impact on the success of the company or its customer base. Thus, the research focus was on the propensity of the SaaS provider's clients to renew their subscription or continue to use the service at a different service level to which they had previously subscribed.

Entrusted with such a unique research opportunity we gave much thought to the research design, eventually coming to the realisation that for this research to be truly encompassing of practical reality we would need to adopt a two-phase approach to the study. In Phase 1, we would start with a quantitative analysis of the real-world CC renewal/ attrition customer exit data set we were given. The intent here was to surface sub-scription attrition performance drivers from the exit data provided by the SaaS subscription company. Guided by previous subscription and renewal research studies, the B2B customer relationship management (CRM) cri-teria, the experience factors exhibited in Fig. 6.2 and our taxonomy pre-sented in Table 6.1, the data self-selected into logical coded groupings based on the influence of the reason type. Once this phase was complete, we intended to follow up on that subset which were influenced by factors other than those that might be considered hard or objective decision cri-teria, as we believed that these decision-making influences might yield valuable practical insights. Our overriding goal was to identify means through which SaaS providers could minimise attrition or maximise rev-enue renewal. Thus, an additional qualitative collection cycle investigat-ing those influencing factors that impact the renewal decision was added to the research plan.

8.2.1   Mining the Data

First we considered the raw data set fields, as summarised in Table 8.1.

Table 8.1   Existing exit survey instrument—raw data

Customer data	Customer value	Renewal actions
Opportunity name	Prior Annual Contract	Forecast category
Opportunity ID	Value (ACV)	Forecasted ACV change $
Account ID	Licence renewal status	Primary competitor
Region	Auto renewal y/n	contract Term
Shipping State/	Opportunity owner	Licence utilisation
province	Prior renewal term	True login rates
Market segment	Prior contract term	Close date
Segment	# Licences	Manager notes
Region		Next steps
Contract end date		

Renewal outcome:
  Reason for Licence Change (RFL)
Outcome history:
  Reason detail (RFL Subreason)
  Locked employees
  Extension

It should be noted that while this data set was gathered at the time of each consumer renewal /attrition decision relating to this company, the data collection instrument was not designed by us. However, as this instrument is focused on the attrition/renewal and influencing factors (Fig. 6.2) that equate to the comparative exercise carried out by us on the taxonomy criteria established earlier in the study (Table 6.1), we believed it was sufficiently close in its design to be fit for use, and of value, to the research process. We were reassured that the studied statistics were both well captured and reportable and that they offered a level of baseline data that was both appropriate and applicable for research purposes. On detailed review of the data outputs of these surveys, we were also satisfied that the database was robust in its management of the captured data. At all times, our primary goal was to establish the reasons offered for cancellation or reduction of the existing subscription. We achieved this goal via analysis of the exit data provided by these subscribers (Table 8.1), noting that the attrition data in the company database was measured both through 'during the fact' exit interactions and via an online survey sent to randomly selected clients once the decision was made and communicated to end the subscription.

8.2.2 Deciding What to Look At?

We set about anonymising the data set (Denscombe 2010) through the removal of all commercially sensitive renewal performance and customer identification data not previously publically available. This important and formal approach was predetermined by the research data (Hair et al. 2000) and it was undertaken to ensure that both the listed subscribers and the participating company were afforded complete anonymity.

One of the early issues to be resolved was the segmentation of the research cohort into meaningful research sample sizes, particularly as we were interacting with a database of 10,000+ subscribers. We paid particular reference to previous research literature. Taking on board the data mining steps recommended by Fayyad et al. (1996), we contemplated anomaly detection, dependency modelling, clustering, classification, regression and summarisation (Fig. 5.1, Chap. 5) in interaction with the data set. This approach allows a search for valuable information in large volumes of data (Weiss and Indurkhya 1998), and should therefore facilitate classification and clustering (Liao et al. 2012).

As an alternate to this technical approach to data mining, we also looked at Ngai et al. (2009) who cite analytical CRM as the basis for identifying customer characteristics and behaviours, so as to support an organisation's customer management strategies. These criteria are discussed in full in Chap. 5. Throughout we benchmarked these alternates to the Miles and Huberman (1994) belief that data reduction is a form of analysis that sharpens, sorts, focuses, discards and organises data in such a way that final conclusions can be drawn and verified. In their different ways, we felt that each of these latter approaches would be applicable to the research undertaking and would support the pursuit of the research question and objectives.

What is the B2B recurring revenue model for the delivery of SaaS through a CC channel?

1. Examine existing software revenue models and assess their applicability to CC SaaS provision.
2. Identify the drivers, risk factors and subscription renewal influences in CC SaaS B2B renewals.
3. Explore the reasons why customers (subscribers) renew, reduce or attrit their SaaS, or CC subscription services.
4. Analyse the renewal criteria applied by B2B clientele.
5. Propose a B2B revenue renewal model for delivery of SaaS through a CC channel.

Thus, for the final data reduction stage, we applied a combination approach in context.

Based on our review of the CC SaaS global market, we believed that the 'average contract value' of specific cohorts was also an important factor in that it indicated that the SaaS subscription was most likely to have been contracted on the expectation that it would be a business value enhancing productivity tool. The decision to purchase, reduce or attrit the subscription was therefore likely to have been given more consideration for this commercial cohort than would, say, the addition or reduction of a consumer product, supporting our earlier decision to focus only on B2B subscribers.

The geographic region of the subscription user also proved to be an important input as the location factor brings many influences on the usage and adoption of the product set, all of which impact on the likelihood of the subscription being renewed (Hosseini and Tarokh 2011). The attractiveness of a service and its subsequent renewal propensity are very different in its home and remote markets (Khajvand and Tarokh 2010). In the home market the product will have attributes, positive or negative, which are uniquely tied to the market in which it is being promoted. These renewal attributes can differ significantly in a remote market, where subjective influences like language and culture alter the renewal landscape. This initially posed a dilemma for us, and we debated whether to include all geographies or to consider a smaller, tighter cohort where the renewal reasoning and data is more constrained and appropriate to measure and analyse. On consideration of the usual limits relating to research (e.g. time and manpower), we agreed that a tighter and closer aligned single-geography and single-segment size research cohort was the most appropriate for this research.

Based on the preceding premise that the attrition or renewal decision in one segment of the database will have fundamentally different objectives and subjective judgements from the attrition or renewal decision in another, we decided that the research would be most valuable if undertaken from the point of view of the B2B subscriber only, and based in the US as the geographic boundary. In Chap. 5, we have already laid out the reasoning for the concentration on the B2B market segment rather than looking at both B2B and (Business-to-Consumer) B2C. For the geographic segmentation, separate from the single-geography, single-segment decision explained above, there was the additional research attractiveness to the US as the chosen geographic region in that it is a region widely acknowledged as being 'tech-savvy', with an open and technologically supported business culture. We further limited the focus to the lower mid-market segment of the subscription base—specifically customers with an Annual Contract Value (ACV) of between \$25,000 and \$100,000. This segment was chosen in that it offered a clearly delineated group of B2B Cloud SaaS subscribers, with a single currency and a single business language and a subscription value point which was significant enough to support multiusers and multiapplication functionality choices.

The final subscriber segment used for the research combines that level of 'stickiness' needed to ensure the attrition business decision is a considered one, that is, the significance of the monetary spend, with a sufficient market share size such that the overall attrition calculations aren't skewed by single, high-value events which might be the case in the higher-end segments.

This data distillation process resulted in a reduction in the initial data set of over 10,000 subscribers down to a sample subset of specific attriting subscribers showing 4159 separate subscriber accounts (Table 8.2).

8.2.3   Deciding What to Look For?

On completion of the data refinement process, we considered it most appropriate to then collate the data based on the provided 'Reasons for Loss' (RFL) codes within the reduced data set (Table 8.3).

The data headings were examined to ensure that the RFL labels were consistent across subscriber records and that every record of the research focus data set included one of the predefined RFL value codes. This provided a logical and consistent basis for the grouping of the RFL data points.

Table 8.2 Data distillation process

Stage	Description	Customer records
1.	Remove commercially sensitive information from the data set	10,000+
2.	Reduce the annual attrition data down to identify only those customers where Annual Contract Value (ACV) is in the range of \$25k–\$100k	6,573
3.	Select only those attriting/reducing customers located within the US business geography	4,159

Table 8.3 Company provided reason for loss (RFL) codes

RFL code	Criteria	Paradigm
Economic	Reduction in Force (RIF), suspended, Chapter 11 (bankruptcy)	Objective
Adoption	Unused licences, never deployed, light functional use	Subjective
Political	Merger + acquisition, sponsorship, policies	Objective
Price concession	Product price change, new corporate price, tiered volume pricing	Objective
Limited life	Short-term licences and services	Objective
Oversold	Transfer of users, wrong product	Objective
Business practices	Change in 'go to market' strategy	Subjective, objective

8.2.4 What Can the Loss Codes Tell Us?

Refined and reduced, it quickly became apparent that the data set was providing both valuable subscription exit data and strong, distinct groupings based on the proffered driver to attrit. The process of subscriber clustering adopted offered an important insight into how the Cloud SaaS provider might measure their clients' renewal decision process, reinforcing the factors framework offered in Chap. 6.

There is a historic leaning in the tracking of subscriber behaviour towards measuring past subscription renewal decisions as a counting exercise and then using the outputs from the count to extrapolate and predict future subscriber behaviour and future buying patterns. This is at odds with the optimised CRM approach articulated in Chap. 5 as quantifying such behaviours in this way is a misnomer. These old style churn predictors may be acceptable in more traditional subscription marketplaces but in the case of true Cloud SaaS subscriptions the measurement of the segment is more refined in that, by its nature, significantly more data and service usage touch points exist in formats technically and commercially easier to collect and collate. CC service providers are now in a position to gather significant historic and real-time data on the usage of their service offerings. If appropriately gathered and retained, this facilitates the attentive industry participant with a unique insight into the consumption and adoption of their subscription offering. Unfortunately, many fail to build the longevity foundation of collecting, tracking, and acting on the ongoing customer buying behaviours which this historic usage data will uniquely give them (Tyrväinen and Selin 2011).

8.2.5 Are All Losses the Same?

The RFL codes map to two distinct and very different paradigms—the soft, qualitative, measures tracked by the Adoption (Usage/Value) and Trust/Satisfaction RFLs and the harder, objective RFL measures like Price and Limited Life which are more appropriately measured in their quantitative form. This was a significant insight in that this natural, and self-selecting, clustering of the exit reasons provided by the reducing subscriber could be grouped either simply as addressable/ non-addressable or, in our viewpoint, in the more meaningful three-way grouping of non-addressable, soft/subjective reasoning and hard/objective reasoning.

Having categorised the RFL in this way (Table 8.4), it is of value to contemplate each grouping in turn.

Table 8.4 Reasons for loss (RFL)

Soft/subjective	Hard/objective	Non-addressable
Usage/value	Price concession	Out of business
Never deployed	Oversold	Bad debt
Unused licences	Business practices	Reduction in Force (RIF)
Light functional use	Limited life licences	Merger and acquisition
Low login	Sold wrong product	Corporate standard
High usage limited	Product price change	Corporate pricing
business value	New corporate price	
Sales Process or	Reverse licence ramp	
contract terms	Bug/product instability	
Poor perceived value	Billing frequency	
Trust/satisfaction	Term extension	
Transfer to Reseller	Tier pricing	
Management change	Multiyear price ramp	
Competitive risk	Transfer of users	
Lack of sponsorship	Product no longer	
Analyst influence	matches needs	
Partner dissatisfaction	Unsuccessful pilot	
	New security policies	
	Foreign exchange	

Non-Addressable Losses

In non-addressable cases, the trigger is either catastrophic, like bank-ruptcy, or outside of the Cloud service provider's control, like customer acquisition or merger. In either situation, the service supplier has the predetermined decision handed to them without being afforded an opportunity to influence it. These situations are not completely without merit though, as these unaddressable losses or attrition reasons can also provide the Cloud service provider with useful key performance indica-tors (KPIs). This is particularly true around the collection of economic loss data, where the failure to maintain the expected renewal rates in a specific market or geography may well be the harbinger of more signifi-cant happenings in the greater economy. For this first grouping of non-addressable loss, we look to the advice of an industry insider interviewed as an expert in the course of this study.

> The Cloud provider response to these non-addressable attrition types should be simple—move on! Nothing commercially reasonable could, or should, be done to save these subscription losses and to invest either time or money in trying to change this is a waste of both (time and money). Instead the Cloud Company should invest in simply trying to predict the event early so as to minimise the financial exposure and revenue shock. Just quantify these as early as possible and hedge against them. Remember Wall Street loves the predictability of a Cloud Company's revenue.

Of interest is that in the case of mergers and acquisitions, all is not lost. In many instances, the merger and acquisition activity can open new sell-ing opportunities for the incumbent supplier, with the combined weight of the new merged business as a continued or new potential buyer of the existing Cloud service. However, it is our view that this is more properly measured as a new business opportunity rather than an existing subscrip-tion renewal, as the merged or acquired entity is no longer the original business. The previous subscription may well have been continued, or even expanded, but the buyer is a different entity and the transaction should be measured as such. To count this growth as part of the overall attrition management results would be to potentially overstate the cus-tomer retention performance levels.

Addressable Loss

Addressable loss is a key business influencer for the CC company and capturing the influence factors affiliate to these RFL is a key element in a sustainable revenue model (see Fig. 6.2). Every reduction in attrition adds value straight to the bottom line of the service provider. It doesn't matter whether this is measured in dollars saved or percentage attrition reduced. It results in the same bottom-line gains—the B2B subscriber will keep paying the service provider the existing revenue for a longer time. The leaky bucket (Exhibit. 6.1) keeps getting filled quicker than it dries out which, simplistically but impermeably, means continued growth and a thriving revenue stream for the service provider.

The renewal statistics provided in the research data are measured through 'after the fact' exit data. This ensures that the statistics on the number of customers renewing or attriting are accurately captured, but this approach does not necessarily allow us to see what is there in narrative form rather than just the cold numbers captured. The grouping of subscriber reasons for renewal or attrition provides a mainly one-dimensional view of the renewal data (Bernstein 1983), which creates something of a research deficit regarding the detailed reasoning behind the attrition action. Therefore, our next step in the research journey was to ask:

> How could we uncover richer data on the renewal thought process so that an industry practitioner can address these influential losses?

From the data set, patterns emerged which allowed us to make groupings of the RFLs collected from the attriting subscriber records. The patterns themselves captured a quantifiable snapshot (i.e. what the actual outcome was) but they provided little insight into the reasons behind the commercial decision. Although this approach successfully records the high-level reasons offered for cancellation or reduction of the existing subscribers via the exit data provided by these subscribers, its weakness is that the data is one-dimensional.

Morgan and Hunt (1994) believe that the decision to renew is fundamentally a subjective one, with many free choice variables in play as influence factors in and of the decision. When the RFL is captured as a piece of exit data without deeper investigation this can miss a significant part of the story in that every renewal or attrition decision is influenced by some external or extraneous event or thinking. Where this upstream influence is driven by a hard, objective measure such as a price point, the Cloud service provider has a straightforward decision or remedial action choice to alleviate the risk. But when the renewal decision is influenced by something not measured as easily as a price point, but by something as nebulous as a lack of company trust, for example, then the challenge for us, and more practically for the industry, is how this influence can be established early enough to allow the service provider to address the attrition risk.

Using the reduced data set, we therefore looked at how the addressable losses of Table 8.4 might lend themselves to further categorisation. Table 8.5 shows our groupings of the potential shortcomings in the

Table 8.5 Analysis of the shortcomings in the existing RFL data codes

Self-inflicted: insufficient customer focus	Self-inflicted: poor internal quality management policies
Price concession	Contract transfer to reseller
Limited life	Transfer of users
Oversold	Management change
Business practices	Sales process or contract terms
Sold wrong product	Product no longer matches needs
Product price change	Consulting, services, support
New corporation price established	Merger and acquisition corporate pricing
Reverse licence ramp-down	
Lack of sponsorship	Partner dissatisfaction
Bug/product instability	New security policies
Billing frequency	Analyst influence
Tier pricing achievement	Foreign exchange
Addressable	**Non-addressable**
Unused licences/poor adoption	Mergers and acquisitions corp standard
Low login rate	Bad debt
Light functional use	Reduction in Force (RIF)
High usage/limited business value	Out of business
Never deployed	Unsuccessful pilot
Not seeing value	Competitive risk

existing RFL data codes. We did this in order to simplify understanding of the attrition influences that might be considered as a means to address these exposures.

Of these groupings, the first two SaaS provider self-inflicted losses (e.g. insufficient customer focus and poor internal quality management policies) would appear, as their grouping name suggests, the easiest for the Cloud company to fix. From a mechanical viewpoint something as simple as a price concession or the frequency with which a subscriber is invoiced is a straightforward operational business change. Further pricing strategy examples and CRM approaches are outlined in Chaps. 4 and 5. This approach may need caution, however, in that for an established Cloud service provider with an existing revenue stream and a public expectation of continued revenue performance, making these minor adjustments at scale can multiply to a significant revenue impact over the longer term. For this reason, identifying these attrition drivers as early as possible in the subscriber life cycle is likely to be important.

Taking the wider customer perspective at Table 8.5, it is clear that some RFL—like price and economic conditions—are very definitely objective and not influenced by subjective forces. But this 'hard' data is only one part of the picture and it doesn't address the more subjectively influenced attrition drivers' data like the subscribers' lack of trust in the provider or their perceived lack of value received (Fig. 6.2). In creating these objective/subjective groupings, we concluded that the renewal, or its opposite—a conscious decision to cancel a subscription—may not be as simple as the binary 'yes' or 'no' that Whitney (1996) believes it is. The final decision communicated may well be the objective binary decision but this hard measure may not always tell the true story of the thought process and influences leading into the renewal decision. These are better examined through a subjective interpretation.

In support of this perspective, we considered the data through the multilens of both objective and subjective reasoning criteria. Having done so we were confident in our findings that to fail to adequately research these subjective drivers would have left a significant shortfall in the research such that it would have produced a much weaker set of findings on which to base our contribution to practice.

8.3 Exploring the Subjective Drivers of the Renewal/Attrition Decision

The grouping process set out above was fruitful in that it provided a definite cluster (Liao et al. 2012) as a basis for analysis in Phase 2 of the research study. This clustering was important in that, in consultation with the relevant literature, it allowed the RFL categories to be further distilled into the two distinct categories of 'hard' or objective RFLs versus those influenced by 'soft' or subjective RFLs. The grouping of the data in this way facilitated the segmentation of the original Phase 1 data set into further subsets of attrition results delineated by objective and subjective attrition influences (Table 8.6). This encouraged a deeper investigation and further analysis of this subset that would look specifically for the subjective drivers that may have influenced the final renewal outcome.

In pursuing an understanding of the subscription user's perspective and considering the factors that influence the renewal process, support for this distillation process came from the literary-influenced taxonomy presented in Table 6.1, Chap. 6. Burez and Van den Poel (2007), Taylor and Hunter (2002), Verhoef (2003) and Peppard (2000) provide the basis for the research instrument design being independent of the pre-existing data.

Table 8.6 Reason for attrition data set

Reason for loss (RFL code)	Number of attritions	Percentage of total (%)	Hard/soft	Phase 2 inclusion
Usage/value	1068	26	Soft	Include
Price concessions	545	13	Hard	Exclude
Data[a]	586	14	Hard	Exclude
Economic/bad debt	378	10	Hard	Exclude
Failed implementation	8	0	Hard	Exclude
Independent Software Vendor (ISV) (partner) failure	410	10	Hard	Exclude
Trust/satisfaction	273	7	Soft	Include
Product	7	0	Hard	Exclude
Self-inflicted	598	14	Hard	Exclude
Uncategorised/no reason	286	6	N/A	Exclude
Total	4,159	100		

[a]Data cleansing product, with inherently lower propensity to renew

As we mined the data set, the attritions influenced by the hard RFLs were those where the decision to renew or attrit is based objectively on a hard, quantifiable measure such as performance against a price point. These RFLs were then compared with the rationale behind the soft, subjective measures such as where the customer subscriber would look at the same price point data not as a binary objective decision, but through the more subjective lens of the perception of value. This data reduction step resulted in 2818 attrition customer records that were classified as being driven by the hard RFLs and the remaining 1341 records driven by soft or subjective RFLs. Thus, we included those 1341 data records, which were viewed as having had a subjective influencer informing the decision to attrit (Table 8.6) in Phase 2 of the study.

This data subset is softer and more open to interpretation through the themes of perceptions of value, usage, trust and satisfaction. These attributes were not initially obvious to us early in our study but were exposed through deeper analysis and study of the data set later in Phase 1. For this subjective subset to be explored successfully in pursuit of the original research question and objectives, the intent behind the soft RFLs would require a more thorough qualitative analysis rather than simply taking the performance outcome at face value. To do this in a meaningful way, we sought to engage with a small representation of this subscriber subset through the completion of a series of semi-structured interviews.

8.4   In the Mind of the Data: What Were B2B Subscribers Thinking?

The research goal was to guide discussions with both randomly selected subscribers from the 1341 subscribers' data set and with Cloud service providers on their perception of the service offerings so as to afford us an understanding of the qualitative drivers behind the attrition decisions (Saunders et al. 2003; Remenyi et al. 2005). We hoped that this would result in a significant contribution to the understanding of the factors impacting the robustness of the SaaS CC subscription model (Sosinsky 2011), such as could then be applied as a practical learning for the Cloud industry.

Commonality across the 1341 subscriber set was that the RFL provided by the subscriber to the initial data collection process was subjective. For a complete understanding of the factors that influenced the renewal decision, we knew we would have to reach out directly to the decision maker to hear from them as to what informed their attrition decision. To ensure a fair representative from this cohort, this soft RFL grouping was also used as the data set input for a randomisation process in preparation for Phase 2 of the research study. We recognised that the subscribers' renewal/attrition lens was guided by a yet to be established subjective influence not obvious from the initial captured data. To uncover this key is to establish whether the subscriber decision process was as objective as the 'price being too high, too low or just right', or, as Morgan and Hunt (1994) believe, that the subscriber decision process was a much more personally subjective issue like the level of trust placed in the service supplier.

For the subscriber interviews, the themes to be explored were identified through engagement with the taxonomy criteria of Table 6.1, the experience factors framework (Fig. 6.2) and the initial B2B SaaS revenue renewal model (Fig. 7.1). In addition, the exit data relating to renewal or attrition decisions extracted from Phase 1 of the research study (Tables 8.3, 8.4, 8.5 and 8.6) contributed to our understanding of the subjective reasons behind a particular subscriber decision. In particular, we acknowledged both the specific criteria that linked the customer to the service provider, such as could be seen as creating a loyalty to the quality of service, and the previous performance of the service provided. Supported by the research literature, we found that such loyalty may be a predictor of customer churn (Kim et al. 2004) or a deeply held commitment to rebuy (Oliver and Bearden 1985). In these cases, loyalty can be conceived of as a 'more important customer consideration than even price' (Reichheld and Schefter 2000), as it amounts to 'what I do' versus 'what I feel' (Morgan 2000) in the subscriber's decision approach. As such, it is included as a key supplier side renewal influence (Zineldin 2006).

Based on a review of relevant literature, particularly the CRM body of work Payne and Prow (2005) and Kim and Yoon (2004), we surmised that as well as pursuing the attrited customers, there was merit in also expanding the interview base to include the views of Cloud industry experts, customer intelligence specialists and data scientists for insight into the relevant research objectives. Based on this insight, we decided it would be prudent to discuss the subjective influencers exposed in our review of the attrition database with the Cloud company's customer data science team and with its customer subscription protection experts. This served to both elicit the company perspective on the concept of subjective criteria identified in Phase 1 as well as expose their view on the customer research response rate. In keeping with Creswell's (2007) approach, we then additionally identified a small group of SaaS and CC pioneers and experienced executives in the sector and further sought to illicit their views through a series of interviews guided by the same topics (Table 8.7).

The selection of these respondents was non-random, reflecting the emergent nature of the research. This approach allowed us to anticipate the need for new interviewees to enable new insight in light of any additional research avenues, which might be highlighted from discussions with the original intended customer cohort, and to select additional interviewees suiting the needs of the research.

We grouped the loyalty factor and those further themes which amounted to the meaningful data patterns of Ritchie and Spencer (2002) and refined these into the 'soft influence' criteria that appeared to have an effect on renewal decisions in interaction with the hard, factual RFL data codes of Table 8.6. Thus, taking cognisance of the Phase 1 data findings, we identified customer perceived value, perceived level of SaaS usage in the subscriber firm, the element of trust, levels of perceived customer satisfaction, previous performance and quality of service and customer

Table 8.7 Non-subscriber interview schedule

No.	Interviewee role	Duration
1	Data scientist	60 minutes
2	Data scientist	70 minutes
3	Customer intelligence specialist	55 minutes
4	Customer intelligence specialist	60 minutes
5	CC subscription provider	90 minutes
6	CC subscription provider	75 minutes
7	CC founder	60 minutes
8	CC industry specialist	45 minutes

loyalty as key themes to be explored with the subscriber, throughout applying a semi-structured interview approach. The outcomes of these interviews are discussed below.

8.4.1   Customer Perceived Value

The RFL data from the input data set included measures on attrition influenced and driven by a value perception change on the part of the subscriber (Dick et al. 1995). This perceptual shift could be negative or positive based on the research findings, and partially drove the decision to renew or attrit. This finding is consistent with Heiman and Muller (1996) who established that customers change their prior views on the product value after sampling it. Guided by the interviewee insights, it is apparent that perceived value was an important evolving entity, which is consistent with the Niculescu and Wu (2011) categorisation of digital goods as being 'experience' goods whose value is learnt by customers.

8.4.2   Perceived Level of SaaS Usage Within the Subscriber Firm

The reason for attrition input data set of Table 8.6 cited 'usage' as another major sectional theme for the RFL trends. Usage, aka adoption, of the Cloud SaaS service is what Chen and Hitt (2002) call a 'good predictor of switching and attrition'. Highlighted from the input RFLs of Table 8.6, it was of significance that, when combined, usage, adoption and value together account for 26% of the attrition recorded yet, at the same time, the reasons provided for the lack of use do not lend themselves to easy quantification. McLauchlin (2010) found that leveraging customer usage analytics helps identify potential attrition issues yet simply quantifying the values recorded contributes little to the reasons why the Usage/Adoption is low. We asked ourselves whether this low adoption was driven by the 'disconfirmation of expectations' (Oliver and Bearden 1985) or by the stochastic approach to customer retention (Lilien et al. 1992), which in this case means can low adoption only be analysed statistically or is it

Table 8.8 Adoption/usage levels as an influencing factor in the renewal decision process

Interviewee	Interview extracts
SaaS subscriber	Adoption … is increasing my sales and revenue. I need to see this increasing. You can't fly a plane blind …
SaaS provider	If nobody is logging on then presumably they are getting no value. But this is only table stakes. If they are logging on it may still be below the value of the system so you have to know what their measure of value is …
Data scientist	… is the easiest of the whole lot to quantify. You can determine the true picture of what's happening in the business (based on adoption/ usage activity). They mightn't like the answer but at least they know the answer …
Customer intelligence specialist	… doesn't matter what measure you put, you should be able to measure whether you have achieved it or not …

possible for suppliers to predict renewal using subscriber adoption levels as a guide? All of these possibilities led us to believe that the attriting or cancelling users' perspective was the key to unlocking this mystery; thus we explored this theme by interacting with the various interviewees (Table 8.8).

8.4.3   The Element of Trust

We knew from experience and our exploration of the existing research that the subscriber decision to renew or attrit is not simply about Value and Usage/Adoption. When we contemplated trust's role in the acceptance of Cloud technologies by business (Weinhardt et al. 2009), we included this theme in our conceptualisation of the supplier–subscriber relationship (Fig. 7.1). Equally, He et al. (2004) believe that trust is regarded as subjective and that measuring trust has become an important question for researchers, one which is not appropriate for quantification by deterministic values alone. When we used this same lens to refer back to the attrition data set, we also found trust to be one of the groupings of RFL put forward as a driver of the attrition experienced (Tables 8.3, 8.4, 8.5 and 8.6). For this reason, we believed it to be of key importance. Our interview findings point to trust as having an influence on adoption but

Table 8.9 Trust as an influencing factor in the renewal decision process

Interviewee	Interview extracts
SaaS subscriber	I trust that you are a trusted advisor to my business. I trust that this is a journey that we are going on together and that you are going to guide me through it.
SaaS provider	Trust is 'was the service there and available through the lifetime of the contract?'
Data scientist	The opposite of trust is measurable in terms of attrition. If a customer doesn't trust us they leave immediately.
Customer intelligence specialist	They feel that you are responsible for their success and trust you to deliver this.

also on system use, and that the impact on usage and perceived value is built upon stakeholder experience (Table 8.9).

Our perception of trust, as influenced by Burez and Van den Poel (2007), was as one where the relationship between the SaaS provider and their subscriber was sufficiently strong for both parties to trust each other. The findings also point to an expectation that the SaaS supplier will work towards supporting the subscriber's business coupled with respect for the subscriber's system needs and pursuit of a mutual business partnership. It is important to note that this perception influenced our approach to the research methodology and design and also significantly impacted any preconceived idea of the relationship the SaaS business had with that subscriber cohort. Specifically, Burez and Van den Poel (2007) view that the trust that exists between the customer-focused SaaS provider and their end user was particularly challenged during this phase of the research, and this challenge became a significant outcome of the research undertaking in its own right.

Of equal importance for this consideration was a contrarian view to the beliefs of Morgan and Hunt (1994) and Rust et al. (2000) that trust is amongst the most prominent influences on a customer's relationship perception. To this end, Verhoef (2003) countered by seeing trust as an antecedent of satisfaction and commitment rather than a direct outcome of its influence. We gave considerable thought to this in light of the research findings, as the seeming conflict of each diverse view could have an impact on how we explored the interview transcripts. Eventually, we came to the acceptance that each opinion simply agrees that trust is impactful on the customer decision and that when combined with trust being recorded as a valid RFL in the input data set together with the interview outcomes, each adds credence to trust being another theme worthy of inclusion as a subjective renewal factor.

8.4.4   Levels of Perceived Customer Satisfaction

As '(dis)satisfaction' relates to customer retention and customer share development, it was also included as a theme for exploration through interview. Bolton et al. (2000) support this belief that satisfaction drives customer retention (and that dissatisfaction leads to attrition) over time. Likewise, we believed that the measure of emotion driving this RFL attrition decision could be realistically perceived as being subjective in nature and, as such, that it would validly merit deeper investigation through the interview process, using the adoption/value theme as a catalyst in context. The interview extracts give insight into the various stakeholder perspectives in context (Table 8.10).

We define satisfaction as the 'emotional state which occurs from a customer interaction with a subscription or service over time' (Verhoef 2003). This interpretation, or rather it's inverse of (dis)satisfaction, also surfaced as a reason offered for dropping or reducing the subscription service from the customer data sample. Dissatisfaction was another of the RFLs recorded in the input data set, and borne out from the detailed interviews, particularly dissatisfaction as it related to customer interaction with a subscription or service over time.

Table 8.10 Satisfaction/adoption as an influencing factor in the renewal decision process

Interviewee	Interview extracts
SaaS subscriber	… it is a conversation not a survey …
SaaS provider	Definitely measurable through usage and through customer success stories
Data scientist	You try to get an understanding of the user measures
Customer intelligence specialist	If (there's) no satisfaction by the foot soldiers then renewal becomes an uphill battle

8.4.5   Previous Performance/Quality of Service

In building the interview themes, neither the perception of previous performance nor the quality of service, as opined by Verhoef (2003) in the original renewal taxonomy (Table 6.1), manifested themselves as valid RFLs in the Phase 1 output data set. While one might have had a reasonable expectation of these being represented in the data set, no such measures, either objective or subjective, were highlighted by the data output. Accordingly this potential research topic, which might have been expected from the taxonomy, was excluded from exploration in the interview schedule.

8.4.6   Customer Loyalty

Much has been made of loyalty as a predictor of customer churn (Kim et al. 2004). Morwitz and Fitzsimons (2004) and Zineldin (2006) champion loyalty and earned brand commitment as key supplier side renewal influences, a factor which Oliver and Bearden (1985) define as a 'deeply held commitment to rebuy'. While this might lead to the expectation that loyalty, or the lack of it, would manifest as a recorded RFL, its absence from the input data set initially surprised us and appeared to contradict Reichheld and Schefter's (2000) argument that loyalty is a more important customer consideration than even price. This fact of loyalty not showing in the RFL offered by the attriting customers was one of particular interest, and reinforces the less popular view that, from a SaaS B2B perspective, loyalty likely equates to Lance Walker's perspective of evidenced repeat purchase (Chap. 5), hence the industry's increasing interest in customer retention and renewal strategies (Woisetschlager et al. 2011).

We looked at the possibility, based on Morgan's (2000) suggestion that loyalty might be measured as the objective behavioural loyalty of 'what I do' rather than the subjective loyalty of 'what I feel' as an appropriate defence, if one was needed. This interpretation, combined with a desire to explore its surprise exclusion fully, led us to actively search for the possibility of loyalty as a theme. Whether explicitly called out as an

Table 8.11 Loyalty as an influencing factor in the renewal decision process

Interviewee	Interview extracts
SaaS subscriber	… if I'm successful I'm significantly more loyal …
SaaS provider	In the SaaS Cloud world, given that it's a young industry, people are loyal because of the thought leadership role you provide. The more you are seen to be a thought leader the wider the loyalty to the brand.
Data scientist	Brand loyalty is more of a factor on initial purchase than on renewal. A repeat purchase is an indication of loyalty. Further purchases of other suites are a better measurement of loyalty. Broadening and deepening the relationship.
Customer intelligence specialist	…but Net Promoter Score (NPS) is not a leading indicator of renewal loyalty in its own right. Negative will definitely tell you are in trouble but positive is only an indication there is no current issue.

RFL or not, we believed it should also be incorporated as an exploratory avenue in the interview schedule, resulting in some interesting insights (Table 8.11).

Having established the renewal influence themes of value, trust, quality, loyalty, adoption and satisfaction, the interviews were structured so as to allow the respondents to provide open, rich descriptions of their renewal experience in their own words. This approach allowed for what Jackson and Trochim (2002) describe as a 'rich description of respondent reality', unconstrained by the segment diversity or geographic dispersal of the sample cohort.

8.4.7 Ambivalence

An unexpected finding from the interview process was what we perceived to be a poor level of engagement from the subscriber base. While the original data set led us to believe that we could expect an animated and motivated interaction from the subscriber base, what we actually found was that the level of interaction was much less engaging than the industry marketing and hype would lead one to expect. Less than 5% of those Cloud subscribers who had dropped or reduced their subscription at the time of renewal were motivated to provide anything other than the objective RFL exit data. Although Cloud service providers pride themselves on being a connected, customer-centric and customer-engaged delivery vehicle, perhaps the exhibited customer engagement ambivalence is a more realistic indicator of the utility-like lens through which many customers view the SaaS provider. Or maybe it simply supports the Groves et al. (1992) belief that the US is being oversurveyed? Sheehan (2001) believes that this oversurveying risks reducing rates of response as 'the aura of uniqueness to the participation in the survey process diminishes'. Thus, the response rate achieved in the SaaS supplier's exit survey among the 10,000+ client data set may well be a valuable finding in its own right.

8.5   Capturing the Views of the Industry

The initial research phases had seemingly clearly created separations between what were segmented as hard, objective and quantifiable measures, as opposed to the others believed to be soft, subjective and unquantifiable. On analysis of the customer transcripts, it became clear that in reality this difference proved to be a misinterpretation. Reviewed in light of the literary themes of adoption, value, loyalty, trust and satisfaction—purposefully separating the customer and expert data in pursuit of fair representation of the different cohorts' perspectives—we found that although many would at first glance appear to be clearly subjective the reality was that each could in fact be measured. Rather than the soft, subjective measures like adoption and value being true, atomic reasons for attrition or reduction, they were simply a manifestation of other, often simpler, objective reasons.

> What surprised me actually is that you put adoption as a subjective measure, right. From my perspective, from what I see, there is a lot of things that are objective that we can't really do anything about, the economic measures right are the things that the Company goes out of business, gets acquired by other companies, these are things that we can't do anything about, right. And you put them in the objective bucket I understand. The subjective one, you put adoption in here which I would usually put in the objective one because it's something which I can measure, right, because they are not using it.

This switch from subjective to objective measures in the RFL decision in the various interviewee responses was consistent enough to prompt us to clarify the results with both the direct subscription service provider's customer data intelligence team and other SaaS providers' customer intelligence specialists through a series of additional interviews. We found that, just like the subscribers, neither the SaaS Company data science team nor the other SaaS customer intelligence specialists saw any significant differential between objective and subjective measures either, so maybe the simple numeric or hard approach to attrition data measurement would suffice after all.

The SaaS provider acknowledged and was aware of the more subjective RFL with the data and customer intelligence specialists having already identified ways of breaking these subjective adoption losses down into component measures, which they were capable of then measuring in the traditional hard data, ways of other objectives codes. For example, the seemingly subjective measure of **adoption** would in their eyes have been seen as objective on the basis that it can be measured in its most basic form simply by whether the service is being used or not. Likewise, the initially subjective weighted value of **loyalty** was again considered through an objective lens by the data specialists, and was measured as simply as by an extrapolation of previous return buying habits.

> Those are also ways of measuring loyalty. In the end, trust, adoption, loyalty all are factors that reduce attrition and make the customer Company more successful. The, really, it all boils down to delivering business value to the customer.

Not even **trust** was accepted as a subjective decision tool, despite our assumption that this was its appropriate categorisation;

> Is trust measurable? Well, the opposite of trust is measurable in terms of attrition. If a customer doesn't trust us they leave immediately because that's the basis of the relationship, so that we can measure the more business processes our customers implement on our platform the more they trust us. Probably that's the only real measure of success for the Company, right, because similar to a bank the more you trust a bank the more money, the more of your money and the more of your processes you put in the

hands of your bank. If I love my bank I put my 401k, my retirement plan, my credit card, checking account, savings account all in the hands of one bank and that's an indication of trust, of the trusted relationship I have with my bank so I guess the success of a software Company with regard to trust would be how widely, the width of adoption within an organization.

Initially, we were guided by the fact that He et al. (2004) and Rust et al. (2000) had each found trust has historically been placed firmly in the subjective business decision grouping. Yet, for the SaaS company specialists, data science has moved beyond the nebulous interpretation themes of the previous marketing/branding methodologies (Day 1976), and instead trust is viewed in their world as something eminently measurable, through the capture of its opposite where 'if a customer doesn't trust us they leave immediately because that's the basis of the relationship' (customer intelligence specialist).

Similar to the subjective measure of trust, Verhoef (2003) sees **satisfaction** as a manifestation of brand and product allegiance and commitment. In doing so it is seen as a key influencer of customer renewal propensity, which is hoped for rather than measured. To the customer intelligence/data science teams, measuring satisfaction is a standard tool of the trade, one that they utilise and measure as a standard business practice. Thus, they believe satisfaction moves to the objective realm under this lens.

Finally, it was the same for **value**, where following the lead from Groth and Dye's (1999) belief that consumers see the perceived value of a service as a major influence of customer expectations, one would expect that for the SaaS customer value would be a key indicator of commitment to their subscription renewal. Again, for the customer intelligence analyst, it is perceived to be no more than a combination of other factors and once these are identified and tracked then their aggregate will combine into a consolidated value measure;

You have to look at it really in this combination of factors and you know the adoption and reduction and attrition risk is not only related to hard metrics around how they use the product, it has to do directly with how easy it is for them (the subscriber) to get value out of the product.

Subjective or not, once the data scientist is presented with the challenge of measuring these indicators, they seek to revert back to the core quantitative data analysis skills propounded by Bryman and Cramer (1994).

8.6   Subjective–Objective Reasons to Renew: An Updated View

Contrary to the direction initially indicated by the prevailing theory and the Phase 1 data, in reality there is little real subjective data indicated through the reasons put forward for the reduction, or attrition, of SaaS subscriptions. What first appears as a subjective decision can be mapped to and measured by quantitative data points, which are routinely tracked by the SaaS provider. These values can be measured, tracked and specifically actioned to reduce their future impact across the SaaS service offering. Strengthened by the interview data indicating customer ambivalence, this finding highlights the learning that there are in fact few, if any, truly subjective measures, and only ultimately objective ones which will masquerade as something different until data-driven evidence unmasks them as data points which can be quantified, albeit by a very tacit and determined analytical approach.

Zeithaml (1988) succinctly positioned **Value** as 'what I get for what I give'. The evidence from customer feedback is that rather than being the soft perception which the first phase of this research positioned, to the SaaS subscriber it still appears to be firmly guided by the hard measures of price propounded by Marx (1910) over a century ago:

> I need somebody who can take what we do, understand what we are trying to accomplish and provide some consulting services on best use cases, best practices, helping to set it up and plug it in, understand our needs and then kinda create the design. And I'd be willing to pay for this, they could bundle that into our fee. [Company name] does that, [Company name] software does that, they are a services and support provider. [Company name] does that, you know there are a number of those companies that we use

who do that and it works. In [Company name] case they just nickel and dime you to death and then don't provide any other value other than selling you more services.

Likewise, our findings point to the same view on **Loyalty,** where rather than the soft, subjective 'attitudinal loyalty' of Reinartz and Kumar (2002), the evidence from the B2B subscriber interviews is that loyalty is still strongly influenced by a price point and that perceived price fairness (Bei and Chiao 2010) has a direct effect on willingness to renew:

I have a friend for nine years and he's been a [Company name] guy true and true and he can't stand the lack of loyalty from [Company name]. He'll even call me and say, hey here's the way to negotiate with them, they've got a special going on right now and if you do this service you can get a discount on that service. It's a whole game that [Company name] plays because they are such a sales driven organization and not a customer driven, loyalty driven organisation.

The mistake may be that some equate willingness to renew to loyalty, which in practice assumes a leap in the subscribers' perception of the supplier–subscriber relationship.

Based on the reasoning of Morgan and Hunt (1994) and Rust et al. (2000), who both consider **Trust** to be amongst the most prominent influences on a customer's relationship, we also expected trust to be a subjective measure, which could not be measured quantitatively. However, from the interview data, in the customer's eyes it is still all about the hard measures, as clearly evidenced by the viewpoint of one customer:

I don't trust them, all they want is the cheque … calling people three months before their subscription is up and saying, hey, if you renew now we'll give you a better deal.

Trickiest of all to reconcile was the view on **Satisfaction**. Where Oliver's (1980) 'model of satisfaction decision' expresses consumer satisfaction as a function of expectation, the reality from the subscriber feedback was very different, with satisfaction instead measured by delivery of a specific set of objective outcomes rather than a stand-alone decision driver in its own right:

> That's exactly a source of satisfaction for me. It's especially having the consistency as a rep that drives satisfaction and loyalty as well and if you can't keep the same rep covering my Company how about keep a file so that at least you know when you call you're not like starting over every time.

In consideration of these customer and specialist findings, Table 8.12 shows how this is subjective to objective transformation maps, and is measured objectively, in the Cloud or SaaS world.

These research outcomes were not what we expected and were challenging to our initial theory-led perspective of there being distinct objective and subjective attrition data drivers. Still not entirely satisfied or fully committed to what transpired above, we decided to further explore these findings. We were fortunate to be granted a further series of face-to-face interviews with two founding pioneers of other significant, established and successful CC subscription providers. These additional conversations provided new data points but most interestingly the additional results also supported the findings from the earlier interviews. This offered rich insights into the mechanisms, which the SaaS providers had both envisaged and purposely employed, to ensure that these seemingly subjective

Table 8.12 Objective measures of subjective intent

Subjective	Objective match	Measurement	Methodology
Trust	Service availability, data protection, usage	Uptime, data privacy	Service-Level Agreements (SLAs), meta-data tracking
Adoption	Usage	Logins, feature access	Meta-data tracking
Satisfaction	Willingness to endorse	CSAT scores[a]	Customer satisfaction surveys, testimonials
Value	Key performance indicator (KPI)	Revenue (US$)	Return on investment (ROI)
Loyalty	Growth, repeat purchases	Additional product purchases, renewal rate	Sales, renewal results

[a]Customer Satisfaction Score; traditional score system for which a respondent has to express his or her satisfaction for a certain topic on a score from 1-5

values could be tracked and measured right from the start of the Cloud service provider/subscriber business relationship:

> If the customer wants to set up an optimal sales process they have to do a, b, c and d. If we can track whether they have done these four steps and if we can ensure or verify that the user interface is easy to use and supports the customer in their tasks and if our software contains the functionality that is required to implement the steps to realize the business process, then from that point on it's probably safe to assume that the customer is happy and will continue using the product.

From the industry perspective, there is a consistent view that no reasons for reducing or attriting a service should be left unanalysed in an objective way. One of the SaaS pioneers went so far as to ensure that one-to-one 'exit interviews' with attriting customers were built on an objective template from the outset to ensure that softer proffered reasons like 'dissatisfaction' or 'perceived lack of trust' were analysed and broken down into harder, objective values like specific perceived 'product functionality shortfalls' or 'service availability issues', which could be both measured and addressed following interview analysis.

8.6.1 Everything Can Be Tracked: Even the Subjective Perspective

Through 'interactive and real-time exit customer conversations', 'online attrited customer "surveys"', 'targeted "at risk" customer reachouts' and adoption/value-focused engagements (customer intelligence specialist), the SaaS providers all believed that they had the capability to proactively track and engage in analysing the principal RFL or reduction offered by their subscribers. Not only were these engagements viewed in terms of influencing potential future renewal/attrition decisions on an individual basis but also, from the Cloud service provider point of view, these subjectively manifested reductions were also continuously used to influence a programme of objective remedies, which could be delivered 'at scale' to their complete customer base.

This supports the view that focusing on and investing in the success of the SaaS customer business is closely correlated to minimised risk of subscriber reduction (Fig. 6.2).

8.6.2   B2B Customer Segmentation Is Important

Additional to the main findings, a side observation which emerged from the interview phase was that this new-found objectivity was not universal in its value measurements. There is a sense of segmentation displayed in the transcripts that although the subjective perceptions could be measured there was no single set of values that would be applied to all. SaaS is the 'ultimate business democracy' (Meeker et al. 2010), but it is this very democracy which makes it so tricky to measure, and predict, the renewability and ultimate robustness of the SaaS revenue model. In any specific business segment, what might be a very valid subjective measurement key (value, trust, satisfaction, loyalty or adoption expectation), can be completely different or irrelevant in another segment, even within the same industry. As one respondent succinctly put it:

> The value measure of the small business owner, writing a personal cheque for the subscription service is totally different for the employee administrator using exactly the same Cloud service in a large, multinational enterprise.

Both service users may be subjectively influenced by their perception of adoption or value but equally both are weighted completely differently in each business segment. As Marston et al. (2011) articulate: 'no one size fits all'.

8.7   Summary of the Research Findings

The aim of this research was to establish a B2B recurring revenue model for the delivery of SaaS through a CC channel. In pursuing this study, we sought out those influences that contribute to the SaaS renewal decision and to explore the reasons why CC SaaS customers actually renew, reduce or attrit their SaaS subscription services.

The principal findings from the research study are:

1. Subscriber churn is a significant risk for the CC SaaS industry.
2. The reasons for subscribers attriting or reducing their Cloud subscriptions must be captured, trended and acted upon.
3. These reasons can be prejudiced by both subjective and objective influences, but ultimately SaaS suppliers believe that all can be measured.
4. The CC SaaS business can mitigate the attrition risk through early life cycle intervention based on the historic RFL recorded.
5. The SaaS subscriber may view the Cloud service provider as a utility.
6. Cloud users and providers view trust in different ways.
7. Customer segmentation plays an important part in the subscriber/provider relationship.

Following the extraction of the key outcomes from the research data, several themes emerge as being particularly appropriate to the CC SaaS industry (Table 8.13).

We considered that each theme merited separate consideration and, supported by the literature, offered the basis for further analysis of the findings displayed. These findings should offer practical applications for the Cloud SaaS industry.

Table 8.13 Extraction of research themes

Theme	Overview
Trust relationship differential	The trusted relationship between the SaaS provider and the SaaS user and how each side views it is essentially different.
Attrition reasons perceived as measurable	Whether attrition is influenced by subjective or objective factors the industry specialists believe that all factors can be measured objectively.
Customer segmentation	The influence of the customer segment on the renewal habits of that segment's cohort is significant.
CC/SaaS as a utility—lifetime value	Whether the SaaS customer relationship is that of a utility subscriber relationship and its impact on lifetime value.

8.7.1   There Is a Trust Relationship Differential

Rust et al. (2000) look on trust as being amongst the most prominent influences on a customer relationship. Our findings question whether a trusting relationship exists between the SaaS provider and the SaaS subscriber and points to a difference between how each side views this relationship. Of note is that there is an expectation of trust emerging as an influence on the subscription renewal habit. However, how trust manifests and whether it is quantifiable is viewed differently by the SaaS subscriber and SaaS provider. For the SaaS subscriber trust is seen as a foundational business relationship value that can be measured by something as simple as pricing 'even-handedness' (equity), while for the SaaS provider the view of subscriber trust is more about being accepted as trusted guardians of the subscriber data or the security and availability of the service instance.

This disconnect appears significant in that the investments which the Cloud provider must make to maintain their perceived positions as trusted suppliers do not equate with how the Cloud subscribers view the benefit from the same measure. Perhaps no different to Plato's Allegory of the Cave, how this appears to the Cloud subscriber may not be a true representation of reality. Is it that the Cloud SaaS provider has been so vigilant in attending to their measure of trust, that is, data security and service availability, that the Cloud subscription user simply doesn't see this as a trust concern and instead measures trust at another, less basic level? This analogy would be consistent with the views proffered by Micah Solomon around customer excellence in the airline industry in Chap. 5.

Like Maslow's (1943) theory of human motivation and to provide a pictorial representation of this trust expectation differential we mapped a similar hierarchy of needs for the CC SaaS industry (Fig. 8.1).

Adopting a simplistic view of the Maslow hierarchy, the mapping of the subscriber needs regarding the industry service gives an indication of the subscriber's initial physiological (a reliable service, available when required) and safety needs (a secure system with user privacy protected) in relation to the SaaS solution. Over time, the subscriber–supplier relationship builds such that belonging needs take effect in the form of trust and potentially loyalty. However, the research data appears to show a

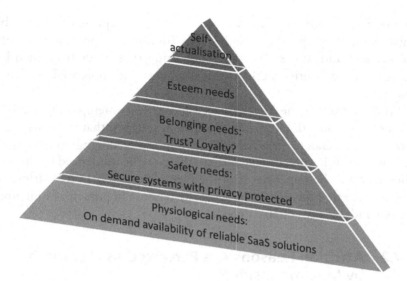

Fig. 8.1 Maslow's hierarchy of needs—SaaS industry (Adapted from Maslow 1943)

'disconnect' between the trust expectations of the subscriber and the supplier, indicating different interpretations of trust for the user and provider. The fact that trust is a consideration when contemplating SaaS renewal at all is perhaps an indicator that the service provider is meeting the foundational service security needs and availability for the Cloud SaaS user (e.g. physiological and safety needs).

Considering trust's role in the customer relationship as evidenced in the research findings, it warrants further discussion. The data shows that trust is a major influence on the subscription renewal habit, as anticipated by Burez and Van den Poel 2007. However, our expectation of trust being a soft, subjective influence on the renewal propensity rather than a hard, quantifiable measure was in part disproved through the research outcomes. This suggests that the SaaS vendor's perception of trust is different from the customer perspective. This is a relevant influence for the Cloud industry to further contemplate, with the research findings additionally showing trust to be an antecedent influence rather than a final outcome. These findings prompt the thought that perhaps Burez and Van den Poel's (2007) perception of measurable trust is industry specific and that this finding is a peculiarity of the Cloud SaaS industry rather than something that holds true for other subscription deliveries. Perhaps this is an area with potential for future research?

Looking back at the hierarchy as a means of contemplating the B2B subscriber's motivation to renew, the findings suggest that these first three levels of the hierarchy (physiological, safety and belonging needs) remain extrinsic needs in this context and can therefore be influenced by the supplier actions. The upper needs of the hierarchy (Fig. 8.1) are intrinsic in nature, such that the user can leverage system use in pursuit of individual esteem and self-actualisation needs.

8.7.2   Attrition Reasons Are Perceived as Measurable by Industry Insiders

The findings provide insight into whether attrition is influenced by subjective or objective criteria and how these influences might be measured. The expectation from Fader and Hardie (2007) was that reasons for attrition, like price and service level, were objective and measurable while others, like trust, adoption, satisfaction, value and loyalty, were subjective and would not lend themselves to being measured in a quantitative way. Both the literature and the taxonomic groupings of the subscription habits (Table 6.1) suggest that while the final recordings of the subscription attrition manifests itself as a hard, objectively driven event, equally it can appear to have been subjectively motivated. Confirmation or otherwise of this hypothesis is of significant importance to the SaaS provider, as any attempt to alleviate attrition would be hampered without clear sight of the true motivation behind the subscriber actions (Fig. 8.1). It was with this in mind that the Phase 2 research cycle specifically sought to investigate this causal relationship and it is of considerable interest that this causal effect is not supported by the research outcomes from the detailed interviews, expert liaison and documentary review.

This finding runs contrary to much of the earlier literature and would suggest that Armbrust et al. (2010) are correct in the assertion that the amount of customer usage data which the CC delivery path makes available to the service provider puts the vigilant Cloud service owner in a uniquely privileged position when it comes to being able to predict the propensity of their customer base to attrit or renew. Similar to the discussion on trust, this finding relates to an industry-specific data benefit rather than one that might carry over into other subscription arenas delivered in a more traditional fashion.

8.7.3 Customer Segmentation Is a Competitive Tool

This theme sought to expose the influence of a customer segment on the renewal habits of that segment's cohort. For the research the attrition data reviewed was purposively chosen as a single-geography, dollar value-delineated B2B subscriber cohort. To have chosen anything more diverse would have risked the overhomogeneity pitfall cautioned by Tsiptsis and Chorianopoulos (2011). This was an appropriate sample size (Bryman 2012) but it also raises the further thought that perhaps a different or wider segmentation might produce different results. Particularly, the views of Frank et al. (1972) point to segmentation as being a major influence on commercial purchasing performance habits, so there may be a valid argument made for the further analysis of the subscription renewal customer lifetime value (CLV) of the Cloud subscriber using the more longitudinal value segmentation proposed by Venkatesan and Kumar (2004) and Rindfleisch et al. (2007). While acknowledging this as a valid path of investigation, we defend our narrower stance on the basis that the customer research data set offered was mandated as being of a single year's value only. Perhaps this finding will encourage other researchers to build on our findings by testing the clues provided by the data that segmentation and CLV are indeed valid further research avenues. No one size fits all and building a Cloud SaaS revenue model on the expectation of a standard renewal rate valid across all segments is now supported by the outcomes of this research.

8.7.4 Cloud Computing/SaaS as a Utility and Its Lifetime Value Impact

This theme revealed that the SaaS customer relationship is that of a utility subscriber relationship, and therefore the industry must consider the utility impact on the relationship. As previously highlighted, as early as the 1960's Kleinrock (1969, as cited in Leiner et al. 1997) believed computer networks would grow in sophistication so that we would see the emergence of computer utilities. In the half-century since, others (e.g. Vacquero et al. 2008; Buyya et al. 2009) have provided technical specifications for computing power delivery, which continue to edge our technical capabilities towards the ubiquitous computing presence. Few would argue against the fact that the utility characteristics (Rappa 2004) have now been matched and delivered by CC SaaS, heralding CC's arrival as the 5th Utility, as detailed in Chap. 3.

The arrival of Cloud SaaS as a utility presents its own business challenges (Armbrust et al. 2010). Separate from the more obvious exposure to customer and subscription churn documented by Kim and Yoon (2004), this baseline prompts a more subtle risk to the industry in that the industry participants will now need to think more like a utility provider in terms of customer relationships and expectations. This links closely with the CLV, customer loyalty and customer longevity expectations and should be considered when thinking about any new revenue model proposed as appropriate for the Cloud SaaS industry. This additional dimension is one that slowly unfolded through the research process, and as such it is now reflected in the forthcoming revenue renewal model (Fig. 9.1) in Chap. 9.

8.7.5 The SaaS 'Value' Debate Should Be Continued

Although mapped separately, what these outcomes serve to underline is that the 'value' debate is as relevant to the Cloud SaaS industry today as it was when first debated in the marketing horizons of Slater and Narver (1994). Seen from the research outcomes and dependent on the viewer's paradigm, value has many faces. Whether value perception by the customer is merely an antecedent of that customer's loyalty, satisfaction and adoption (Lam et al. 2004) or is measured by the Cloud SaaS provider as its next source of competitive advantage (Woodruff 2004), this research data and the literature are at one in highlighting that the perception of value, and delivery against that perception, is a key influencer on the renewal, or not, of the Cloud SaaS licence.

For the Cloud SaaS provider this research outcome raises the question of what should be perceived or measured as customer value and how should the provider expect this value to manifest? Importantly, the interpretation of value differs significantly from that which might have previously been expected from the literature (Venkatesan and Kumar 2004) in that for both the SaaS subscriber and the SaaS provider value is quantifiable and central to the renewal decision (McLauchlin 2010). That both have definite and different measures of value moves the value debate itself from the generic expectations of Zeithaml (1988) to a new place where both the Cloud subscribers' return on investment (ROI) measure and the Cloud service providers' measure of feature consumption (adoption) need to be measured and adjudicated on a continuum rather than as a point in time snapshot. This finding is at odds with the month-to-month subscription model advised by early Cloud SaaS business literature (Armbrust et al. 2010; Ojala and Tyrväinen 2012). It is our view that, based on this study's research findings, and the proposed SaaS revenue model, this monthly flexibility should be put aside in favour of the CLV measures championed by Venkatesan and Kumar (2004) and Rindfleisch et al. (2007).

While the concept of lifetime value is nothing new (Slater and Narver 1994), its applicability to the Cloud SaaS is especially appropriate and, we would opine, uncomfortable. From its very earliest manifestations the CC or SaaS industry has championed the 'dial up' or 'dial down' flexibility of monthly subscription licencing but the reality of lifetime value creation is such that longevity of the subscriber relationship is likely to be a key component of the original (Fig. 7.1) and refined (Fig. 9.1) SaaS revenue renewal model. Like the trust debate above, this theme prompts similar opinions around whether these value expectations and measurements are specific to the Cloud SaaS industry. The literature shows lifetime value had been considered long before the advent of the Cloud but the data outputs from this research would caution that it may well be more important to the industry than might at first glance be expected.

8.8   Conclusion

In summary, all the Cloud SaaS service providers positioned this mapping of subjective intent onto objective outcomes as their key business intelligence value. In an industry that perceives itself as being customer centric (Chowhan and Saxena 2011; Meeker et al. 2010), with a proffered CRM model driving the industry's logic for creating and commercialising value (Osterwalder and Pigneur 2010), customer focus is key (Chen et al. 2011). This view is at odds with our research findings. In reality, there appears little difference between the CC industry and the other four utilities highlighted by Buyya et al. (2009) in that it appears to carry the same customer ambivalence issues that these utilities have experienced in the past. Of course, the Cloud industry, in its current manifestation, cares about its subscriber base but this is often a one-directional care relationship. Now that the industry is increasingly viewed as an expected 'always on' utility (Agyapong 2011) its customer base will expect the connected relationship changes to become utilitarian. If SaaS, or its latest manifestation, CC, does continue on the successful trajectory that Meeker et al. (2010) predict for it, then perhaps this growth comes at the price of converting the fanatically loyal customer base, which Armbrust et al. (2010) believe the industry might reasonably aspire to, to the generally more agnostic, disloyal and promiscuous customer, which Lewis (2002) believes is a prevalence of the true utility service consumer community.

References

Agyapong, G. (2011). The effect of service quality on customer satisfaction in the utility industry–A case of Vodafone (Ghana). *International Journal of Business and Management, 6*(5), 203–210.

Armbrust, M., Fox, A., Griffith, R., Joseph, A., Katz, R., Konwinski, A., Lee, G., Patterson, D., Rabkin, A., Stoica, I., & Zaharia, M. (2010). A view of Cloud computing. *Communications of the ACM, 53*(4), 50–58.

Bei, L.-T., & Chiao, Y.-C. (2010). An integrated model for the effects of perceived product, perceived service quality, and perceived price fairness on consumer satisfaction and loyalty. *Journal of Consumer Satisfaction, Dissatisfaction and Complaining Behaviour, 14*, 125–140.

Bernstein, R. J. (1983). *Beyond objectivism and relativism: Science, hermeneutics and praxis.* Philadelphia: University of Pennsylvania Press.

Bolton, R., Kannan, P., & Bramlett, M. (2000). Implications of loyalty program membership and service experiences for customer retention and value. *Journal of the Academy of Marketing Science, 28*(1), 95–108.

Bryman, A. (2012). *Social research methods.* Oxford: Oxford University Press.

Bryman, A., & Cramer, D. (1994). *Quantitative data analysis for social scientists.* London: Taylor and Frances/ Routledge.

Burez, J., & Van den Poel, D. (2007). CRM at a pay-TV company: Using analytical models to reduce customer attrition by targeted marketing for subscription services. *Expert Systems with Applications, 32*(2), 277–288.

Buyya, R., Yeo, C. S., Venugopal, S., Broberg, J., & Brandic, I. (2009). Cloud computing and emerging IT platforms: Vision, hype, and reality for delivering computing as the 5th utility. *Future Generation Computer Systems, 25*(6), 599–616.

Chen, P.-Y., & Hitt, L. (2002). Measuring switching costs and the determinants of customer retention in internet-enabled businesses: A study of the online brokerage industry. *Information Systems Research, 13*(3), 255–274.

Chen, J., Wang, C., Zhou, B. B., Sun, L., Lee, Y. C., & Zomaya, A. (2011). Tradeoffs between profit and customer satisfaction for service provisioning in the Cloud. In *Proceedings of the 20th International Symposium on High Performance Distributed Computing* (pp. 229–238). New York: ACM.

Chowhan, S., & Saxena, R. (2011). Customer relationship management from the business strategy perspective with the application of Cloud computing. *The Proceedings of DYNAA, 2*(1), 28–38.

Creswell, J. W. (2007). *Qualitative inquiry and research design, choosing among five approaches.* London: Sage.

Day, G. S. (1976). A two-dimensional concept of brand loyalty. In *Mathematical models in marketing* (pp. 89–89). Berlin Heidelberg: Springer.

Denscombe, M. (2010). *The good research guide for small-scale social and research projects* (4th ed.). New York City: McGraw-Hill Open University Press.

Dick, A., Jain, A., & Richardson, P. (1995). Correlates of store brand proneness: Some empirical observations. *The Journal of Product and Brand Management, 4*(4), 15–22.

Fader, P. S., & Hardie, B. (2007). How to project customer retention. *Journal of Interactive Marketing, 21*(1), 76–90.

Fayyad, U., Piatetsky-Shapiro, G., & Smyth, P. (1996). From data mining to knowledge discovery in databases. *American Association of Artificial Intelligence, 17*(3) Fall, 37–54.

Frank, R. E., Massy, W. F., & Wind, Y. (1972). *Market segmentation*. Englewood Cliffs: Prentice-Hall.

Groth, J. C., & Dye, R. T. (1999). Service quality: Perceived value, expectations, shortfalls, and bonuses. *Managing Service Quality: An International Journal, 9*(4), 274–286.

Groves, R. M., Cialdini, R. B., & Couper, M. P. (1992). Understanding the decision to participate in a survey. *Public Opinion Quarterly, 56*(4), 475–495.

Hair, J. F., Robert, P. B., & Ortinau, D. J. (2000). *Marketing research: A practical approach for the new millennium*. Boston: Irwin Professional Publishing.

He, R., Niu, J., Yuan, M., & Hu, J. (2004). A novel Cloud-based trust model for pervasive computing. *Fourth International Conference on Computing and Information Technology proceedings*, Wuhan, China, Sept 14–16.

Heiman, A., & Muller, E. (1996). Using demonstration to increase new product acceptance: Controlling demonstration time. *Journal of Marketing Research, 33*, 422–430.

Hosseini, B., & Tarokh, N. (2011). Customer segmentation using CLV elements. *Journal of Service Science and Management, 4*(3), 157–165.

Jackson, K., & Trochim, W. (2002). Concept mapping as an alternative approach for the analysis of open-ended survey responses. *Organizational Research Methods, 5*(4), 307–336.

Khajvand, M., & Tarokh, M. J. (2010). Estimating customer future value of different customer segments based on adapted RFM model in retail banking context. *Procedia Computer Science, 3*, 1327–1332.

Kim, H.-S., & Yoon, C.-H. (2004). Determinants of subscriber churn and customer loyalty in the Korean mobile telephony market. *Telecommunications Policy, 28*(9), 751–765.

Kim, M.-K., Park, M.-C., & Jeong, D.-H. (2004). The effects of customer satisfaction and switching barrier on customer loyalty in Korean mobile telecommunication services. *Telecommunications Policy, 28*(2), 145–159.

Lam, S. Y., Shankar, V., Erramilli, M. K., & Murthy, B. (2004). Customer value, satisfaction, loyalty, and switching costs: An illustration from a business-to-business service context. *Journal of the Academy of Marketing Science, 32*(3), 293–311.

Leiner, B. M., Cerf, V. G., Clark, D. D., Kahn, R. E., Kleinrock, L., Lynch, D. C., Postel, J., Roberts, L. G., & Wolff, S. S. (1997). The past and future history of the Internet. *Communications of the ACM, 40*(2), 102–108.

Lewis, P. (2002). The psychology affecting loyalty of electricity and gas customers. *The Global Energy Marketing Conference.* Finland: University of Vaasa.

Liao, S.-H., Chu, P.-H., & Hsiao, P.-Y. (2012). Data mining techniques and applications–A decade review from 2000 to 2011. *Expert Systems with Applications, 39*(12), 11303–11311.

Lilien, G., Kotler, P., & Moorthy, K. (1992). *Marketing models.* Englewood Cliffs: Prentice-Hall.

Linstone, H. (1985). Multiple perspectives: Overcoming the weaknesses of MS/OR. *Interfaces, 15*(4), 77–85.

Marston, S., Li, Z., Bandyopadhyay, S., Zhang, J., & Ghalsasi, A. (2011). Cloud computing—The business perspective. *Decision Support Systems, 51*(1), 176–189.

Marx, K. (1910). *Value, price, and profit.* Chicago: CH Kerr and Company.

Maslow, A. H. (1943). A theory of human motivation. *Psychological Review, 50*, 370–396.

McLauchlin, J. (2010). Retaining customers: It's not just about the renewal. *The Marketer, 17*(1), 1–3.

Meeker, M., Pitz, B., & Fitzgerald, B. (2010). http://211.157.29.42/F10Data/HYBG_NEW/DOC/180.pdf. Accessed Aug 2016.

Miles, M., & Huberman, A. (1994). *Qualitative data analysis: An expanded sourcebook* (2nd ed.). Thousand Oaks: Sage Publications Ltd.

Morgan, R. P. (2000). A consumer-orientated framework of brand equity and loyalty. *International Journal of Market Research, 42*(1), 65–78.

Morgan, R., & Hunt, S. (1994). The commitment-trust theory of relationship marketing. *The Journal of Marketing, 58*, 20–38.

Morwitz, V., & Fitzsimons, G. (2004). The mere-measurement effect: Why does measuring intentions change actual behaviour? *Journal of Consumer Psychology, 14*(1–2), 64–74.

Ngai, E., Xiu, L., & Chau, D. (2009). Application of data mining techniques in customer relationship management: A literature review and classification. *Expert Systems with Applications, 36*(2), 2592–2602.

Niculescu, M. F., & Wu, D. J. (2011). *When should software firms commercialize new products via freemium business models.* [Internet] Available at: https://www.misrc.umn.edu/workshops/2011/fall/MariusFlorinNiculescu_2.pdf. Accessed Sept 2016.

Ojala, A., & Tyrväinen, P. (2012). Revenue models in Cloud Computing. *Proceedings of 5th Computer Games, Multimedia & Allied Technology Conference.* GSTF.

Oliver, R. L. (1980). A cognitive model of the antecedents and consequences of satisfaction decisions. *Journal of Marketing Research, 17*(4), 460–469.

Oliver, R. L., & Bearden, W. O. (1985). Disconfirmation processes and consumer evaluations in product usage. *Journal of Business Research, 13*(3), 235–246.

Osterwalder, A., & Pigneur, Y. (2010). *Business model generation: A handbook for visionaries, game changers, and challengers.* Hoboken: Wiley.

Payne, A., & Prow, P. (2005). A strategic framework for customer relationship management. *Journal of Marketing, 69*(4), 167–176.

Peppard, J. (2000). Customer relationship management (CRM) in financial services. *European Management Journal, 18*(3), 312–327.

Rappa, M. A. (2004). The utility business model and the future of computing services. *IBM Systems Journal, 43*(1), 32–42.

Reichheld, F., & Schefter, P. (2000). E-loyalty. *Harvard Business Review, 78*(4), 105–113.

Reinartz, W., & Kumar, V. (2002). The mismanagement of customer loyalty. *Harvard Business Review, 80*(7), 86–95.

Remenyi, D., Williams, B., Money, A., & Swartz, E. (2005). *Doing research in business and management: An introduction to process and method.* London: Sage.

Rindfleisch, A., Malter, A. J., Ganesan, S., & Moorman, C. (2007). *Cross-sectional versus longitudinal survey research: Concepts, findings, and guidelines.* Institute for the Study of Business Markets, Pennsylvania State University, ISBM Report 2-2007.

Ritchie, J., & Spencer, L. (2002). Qualitative data analysis for applied policy research. *The Qualitative Researcher's Companion, 573,* 305–329.

Rust, R., Zeithaml, V., & Lemon, K. (2000). *Driving customer equity: How customer lifetime value is reshaping corporate strategy.* New York: The Free Press.

Saunders, M., Lewis, P., & Thornhill, M. (2003). *Research methods for business students* (3rd ed.). London: Prentice Hall.

Sheehan, K. (2001). E-mail survey response rates: A review. *Journal of Computer-Mediated Communication, 6*(2), 1–14.

Slater, S. F., & Narver, J. C. (1994). Market orientation, customer value, and superior performance. *Business Horizons, 37*(2), 22–28.

Sosinsky, B. (2011). *Cloud computing bible.* Hoboken: Wiley Publishing.

Taylor, S. A., & Hunter, G. L. (2002). The impact of loyalty with e-CRM software and e-services. *International Journal of Service Industry Management, 13*(5), 452–474.

Tsiptsis, K., & Chorianopoulos, A. (2011). *Data mining techniques in CRM: Inside customer segmentation.* Chichester: Wiley.

Tyrväinen, P., & Selin, J. (2011). How to sell SaaS: A model for main factors of marketing and selling software-as-a-service. In *International Conference on Software Business (ICSOB)* (Lecture Notes on Business Information Processing (LNBIP), Vol. 80, pp. 2–16). Berlin/Heidelberg: Springer.

Vacquero, L. M., Rodero-Marino, J., Caceres, J., & Lindner, M. (2008). A break in the Clouds: Towards a Cloud definition. *ACM SIGCOMM Computer Communication Review, 39*(1), 50–55.

Venkatesan, R., & Kumar, V. (2004). A customer lifetime value framework for customer selection and resource allocation strategy. *Journal of Marketing, 68*(4), 106–125.

Verhoef, P. C. (2003). Understanding the effect of customer relationship management efforts on customer retention and customer share development. *Journal of Marketing, 67*(4), 30–45.

Weinhardt, C., Blau, B., & Stober, J. (2009). Cloud computing—A classification, business models, and research directions. *Business & Information Systems Engineering, 1*(5), 391–399.

Weiss, S. M., & Indurkhya, N. (1998). *Predictive data mining: A practical guide.* The Morgan Kaufmann series in data mining systems. San Francisco: Morgan Kaufmann Publishers.

Whitney, J. (1996). Strategic renewal for business units. *Harvard Business Review, 74*(4), 84–98.

Woisetschlager, D. M., Lentz, P., & Evanschitzky, H. (2011). How habits, social ties, and economic switching barriers affect customer loyalty in contractual service settings. *Journal of Business Research, 64*, 800–808.

Woodruff, R. B. (2004). Customer value: The next source for competitive advantage. *Journal of the Academy of Marketing Science, 25*(2), 139–153.

Zeithaml, V. (1988, July). Consumer perceptions of price, quality, and value: A means-end model and synthesis of evidence. *Journal of Marketing, 52*, 2–22.

Zineldin, M. (2006). The royalty of loyalty: CRM, quality and retention. *Journal of Consumer Marketing, 23*(7), 430–437.

9

Recurring Revenue Model, Recommendations and Next Steps

9.1 Introduction

The focus of the book was to study Cloud Computing (CC) and the revenue expectation of the Software as a Service (SaaS) industry, particularly its dependency on the management of its renewal subscriptions (Skilton and Director 2010) to sustain its revenue model. The research sought to establish those influences that contribute to the SaaS renewal decision and to explore the reasons why CC SaaS customers actually renew, reduce or attrit their SaaS subscription services. In doing so it focused especially on the delivery of SaaS through the CC channel, in the Business-to-Business (B2B) domain.

In supporting this research question, this book sought to identify existing business models and considered their applicability in context. The resultant conceptual model exhibiting B2B recurring revenue for delivery of SaaS through a CC channel offers a baseline from which to study the concept in practice. An analysis of real-world attrition and reasons for loss (RFL) data captured from a 10,000+ Cloud SaaS B2B subscriber base provided a basis for the book premise and its underlying research question. We investigated the drivers, risk factors and

© The Author(s) 2018
D. Dempsey, F. Kelliher, *Industry Trends in Cloud Computing*,
https://doi.org/10.1007/978-3-319-63994-9_9

subscription renewal influences in CC SaaS B2B renewals through a mapping to real-world RFL data analysis. From here, we explored the reasons why customers renew, reduce or attrit their SaaS, or CC subscription, services and analysed the renewal criteria applied by B2B clientele.

Enhanced by the learning from the research outputs and supported by the literature, the initial conceptual model (Fig. 7.1, replicated here for ease of reference) was used to support the documented study and serves as the foundation for the refined recurring revenue model.

There were three key findings from the research, each somewhat different than the envisaged outcomes exhibited in Fig. 7.1.

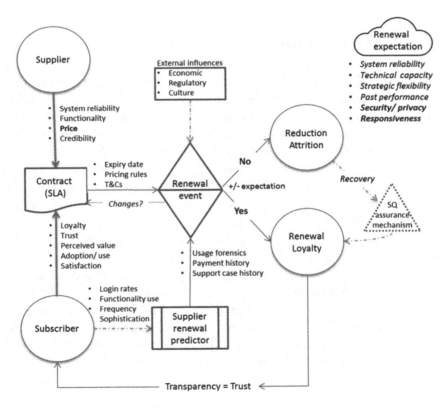

Fig. 7.1   (replica): Initial B2B SaaS revenue renewal model

1. In an industry that is perceived to be customer centric (Chowhan and Saxena 2011), the response rates received from the surveyed cohort indicate a relationship ambivalence closer to that of a utility (Agyapong 2011). This has implications for the customer lifetime value (CLV) expectations inherent in the CC SaaS business model (Osterwalder and Pigneur 2010).

2. The perceived subjectivity of the SaaS attrition or reduction decisions (Walther et al. 2013) is less impactful than might have been expected prior to the study. The SaaS provider's capability of analysing and tracking meta-data usage patterns (Wohl 2008) enables them to track subjective influences through a somewhat counter-intuitive but objective set of algorithms. This outcome can provide the assurance to the SaaS provider that their business foundation is less exposed to unmeasurable customer influences than might previously have been expected.

3. These findings, combined with and strengthened by the study's interview data further highlights a key learning that, within the CC SaaS B2B industry, what could or should be measured as value has different interpretations for both the provider and the subscriber.

In terms of their practical application, these findings mean that the reality of protecting the subscriber base over time becomes a key factor in maximising lifetime value and revenue. Historically all subscriptions are exposed to churn (Kim and Yoon 2004) but none previously had the level of customer interaction and usage data that the Cloud service provider now has. This offers new opportunities for generating customer value in pursuit of their subscription renewal and, in turn, their earned revenue over the customer's lifetime value.

9.2 B2B Recurring Revenue Model for SaaS Providers

Many of the criteria exhibited in the original model (Fig. 7.1) still hold true. Nonetheless, based on the research findings and resultant themes, we believed that some adjustments were required and these are applied to the refined model (Fig. 9.1).

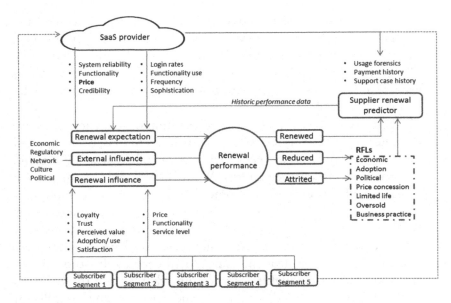

Fig. 9.1   B2B SaaS revenue renewal model

Initially the achievement or otherwise of the renewal event was viewed as a stand-alone event rather than as just a single component on an ongoing relationship continuum. Now it is obvious that the business value is accrued not just from the single renewal event but from many of them over the relationship lifetime so the refined B2B SaaS revenue renewal model (Fig. 9.1) also shows longitudinal awareness of the decision cycle.

The model also needs to anticipate that the customer relationship between the Cloud SaaS provider and the Cloud subscriber might well be one of a utility service user. This alters the industry–consumer power position when measured using Porter's (1980) five forces of competitive analysis guidelines. The utility landscape would leave the Cloud service provider in a somewhat weakened and exposed position if it were not to acknowledge and address this potential subscriber power play in context.

The original model (Fig. 7.1) fails somewhat in addressing the need for a segmented approach to the SaaS supplier's customer base. This is an important learning prompted by the research outcomes. The B2B SaaS recurring revenue model therefore incorporates this segmentation principle to offer the robustness required by Osterwalder and Pigneur (2010) to reflect this segmented business reality.

The perception from the Cloud SaaS subscribers and industry specialists that everything can be measured is particularly relevant to the recurring revenue model. Its inclusion within the revised model is a fundamental enhancement to the original thinking, encompassed in a perpetual circuitry.

A unique feature of the Cloud SaaS industry is the fact that its virtual configuration empowers the service provider through the electronic gathering of significant customer consumption and usage data (Armbrust et al. 2010). By their nature, RFL are historic data points and, when captured after the fact, they are beyond recovery. For the Cloud business provider to create business value from this rich data source, the learning must be transformed into future corrective actions to be fed upstream in the renewal's life cycle to minimise their reoccurrence. This feedback loop was missing from the original model.

As in the previous iteration of the proposed B2B Cloud SaaS revenue renewal model (Fig. 7.1), this refined model highlights the interactions between the Cloud SaaS subscriber and the service provider. Although there is refinement to the original thinking based on the research findings, we believe that the model continues to place renewal performance as the ultimate measure of the Cloud SaaS provider/subscriber relationship and, as such, is at the core of the organic renewal system (Fig. 9.1).

Finally, where the refined model also differs is in the presentation of the renewal influences and expectations as prior considerations that manifest throughout the subscription life cycle rather than simply at the time of the renewal event. The refined model forms a valid blueprint for the Cloud provider and highlights the interface touch points between the renewing subscriber and their service provider. For the Cloud service provider, the model now includes those influences that have the capacity to impact on the success of their renewal transactions. The flow of Fig. 9.1 highlights that the performance of any renewal event has the three distinct sources of influence, namely internal influences, Cloud subscriber perception (titled renewal influence) and external influence. These influences also emulate the original taxonomy (Table 6.1, Chap. 6) drawn from literature and set out in the first stages of this research study.

9.3 Recommendations for Practitioners

These outcomes offer valuable learning to both the CC SaaS practitioner specifically and the CC industry in general. To the practitioner it provides what we believe to be the first large-scale study of practical performance data on the specific subject of CC SaaS attrition management. The relative newness and recent rapid expansion of CC as a go-to-market vehicle for software vendors mean that many incumbents are recent entrants or converts to this business paradigm of subscription pricing and delivery. Because of this, relatively few Cloud businesses of significance have reached that stage of maturity where subscription renewals or attrition has been an area of focus. This has created a ground swell of companies who are now waking up to the realisation that they must understand and control their subscribers' renewability, and do so quickly, if they wish to sustain their revenue model.

In the outputs of the research presented in this book, CC companies will find a subscription revenue model and renewals roadmap which will both guide them as to the importance of the renewal decision and provide them with a template by which to measure and track their attrition exposure. For the practitioners tasked with delivering this key business function within their own CC SaaS business, such a toolset will provide a unique and reassuring pathway to building out their own subscription renewals efforts, offering valuable insights and guidelines for implementation within their business world.

The traditional software industry business model expectation of upfront licence fees and ongoing annual maintenance revenue is not appropriate for the SaaS marketplace. Within the new SaaS business world, if the SaaS provider does not control and minimise its customer and revenue churn, it will initially fail to thrive and ultimately fail to survive. The taxonomy of subscription renewal habits at Table 7.1 (Chap. 7) determines a link from the current SaaS marketplace to the historical practical and academic learning established around earlier manifestations of subscription services. The CC SaaS provider should thoroughly examine the lessons learned by these earlier subscription providers and build on these insights to establish a churn mitigation policy tailored to the latest manifestation of this old style business challenge. It is possible to measure the reasons why SaaS subscribers reduce or attrit their subscription services. These measurements can be mapped using the RFL established in this and other studies. Any effort to protect against, or reduce, the impact of these identified attrition risks should use the historical antecedents of the RFL identified and feed this upstream in the customer life cycle as the basis for their remedy and a protection against their reoccurrence in the future. Reasons for attrition are both objectively and subjectively influenced. However, reasons for reduction or attrition that first manifest as being subjectively distinct are frequently objectively influenced. The subjective drivers can manifest as antecedent rather than final RFL and access to the functional and data usage of the subscriber can both inform and protect the CC SaaS provider's exposure to the impact of both churn influences.

9.4 Closing Thoughts

For CC SaaS to be really understood as a basis for the transformation of the traditional software industry it requires that its description be thoroughly set out within the academic literature and theoretical base as well as in the practice arena. The subscription renewal taxonomy at 7.1 sets out clearly that the expectation of the renewal performance is one that can be both mapped and measured. As the research highlighted, the expectation is that the cause of any non-renewal or renewal reduction could be both identified and mitigated. The identification of the reasons for non-renewal extracted from the SaaS provider's input data set were sufficiently clear to link back to the original taxonomy mapping and once this was done, they could then be meaningfully grouped into objective and subjective causes or influences. This mapping was robustly tested throughout the detailed research phases with the formal interview outputs confirming that the mappings were both theoretically valid and practically applicable.

A primary differentiator of the SaaS provider when compared with the traditional software provider is that the SaaS company is the host of the service used. This gives the service provider a unique overview of the consumption and usage patterns of their customers, a knowledge resource that was previously unavailable in the software industry. Rather than being reliant on the hope that its licenced software was being consumed, as was the case historically, now the CC SaaS provider can see at meta-feature function level what aspects of its service are most attractive to its user base. This uniquely allows the provider to both measure this usage and use this measurement to proactively prompt its greater or wider consumption if required. By combining these usage patterns at an amalgamated level the SaaS provider can strengthen weak service consumption prior to the renewal cycle such that once within that cycle the customer is already solidified on the service adoption track and will likely have a greater propensity to renew the service.

Building on these findings, we believe this work will add considerably to the industry-informed knowledge base for the practice, not just for existing Cloud industry businesses but also for those aspiring new market entrants seeking an insider view of the realities of the global commercial opportunities which SaaS offers now and into the foreseeable future. For the industry, their commercial applicability will be particularly important as the incumbents mature to a stage where the attrition losses from their existing subscriber base have the potential to overwhelm their ability to acquire additional replacement customers at an equal or greater level in order to sustain their revenue model.

9.5   Further Research Avenues and Next Steps for the Industry

This research was undertaken as a 'rear view mirror' analysis. As such, it looked through the data of past events in seeking to clarify subjective thinking. The research outcomes were such as to disprove the secondary pointers of the initial research phases, as guided by the literature, which indicated that attrition data could be broken down into both objectively and subjectively influenced groupings. Clear as these findings are, nonetheless, we feel that, as Pope et al. (2000) point out, sometimes there is a need to revisit, refocus and retest the data elsewhere. Thus, we would recommend that similar research be carried out in the same Cloud or SaaS areas by others such that collectively we can build a multifacilitated view of the industry.

To those researchers who are attracted to the intriguing challenge of even greater understanding of CC and its revenue expectancies, this book will hopefully both provide the encouragement to do so and serve as a basis on which to continue to build the CC SaaS knowledge base. This first step in understanding the CC industry trends in the hopes of eliciting a holistic view of the B2B revenue models is simply that, a first step, but one that hopefully urges many more studies to be taken along the same research path. Those contemplating research in this domain may consider:

- The measurement of the renewal performance and influences across both market and product segments, and perhaps even the consideration of whether some segments are simply not profitable for the CC SaaS service provider to be in.
- That the data cohort provided for this research offers different interpretations of trust and loyalty for the user and provider, such that the consumer then seeks to have a higher level of need met as their baseline trust or loyalty measure.
- The clues provided by the data that segmentation and lifetime value are relevant influences in the renewal decision process provide valid further research avenues.
- The perception of measurable trust as an industry-specific outcome rather than something that holds true for other subscription deliveries warrants further consideration.

Future research could also be undertaken not by measuring the 'after the fact' results as in this case but rather might undertake what Armbrust et al. (2010) label CC subscriber acquisition criteria. In doing so, any future research might undertake a similar study on the influence of the SaaS or Cloud brand value and loyalty but in this instance on pre-acquisition prospects rather than on attrited or reducing existing customers' renewal decisions. Based on our experiences of the current study as 'insiders' in the industry, perhaps this future study would be better carried out by those external to the data cohort or industry.

Irrespective of the motivation to research this domain, our firmly held view is that CC is both a business paradigm with miles to run and an academic field with many opportunities for exciting and fruitful research. We wish future researchers the same exciting journey as we found ourselves on as this industry review unfolded!

References

Agyapong, G. (2011). The effect of service quality on customer satisfaction in the utility industry—A case of Vodafone (Ghana). *International Journal of Business and Management, 6*(5), 203–210.

Armbrust, M., Fox, A., Griffith, R., Joseph, A., Katz, R., Konwinski, A., Lee, G., Patterson, D., Rabkin, A., Stoica, I., & Zaharia, M. (2010). A view of cloud computing. *Communications of the ACM, 53*(4), 50–58.

Chowhan, S., & Saxena, R. (2011). Customer relationship management from the business strategy perspective with the application of cloud computing. *The Proceedings of DYNAA, 2*(1), 28–38.

Kim, H.-S., & Yoon, C.-H. (2004). Determinants of subscriber churn and customer loyalty in the Korean mobile telephony market. *Telecommunications Policy, 28*(9), 751–765.

Osterwalder, A., & Pigneur, Y. (2010). *Business model generation: A handbook for visionaries, game changers, and challengers*. Hoboken: Wiley.

Pope, C., Ziebland, S., & Mays, N. (2000). Qualitative research in health care: Analysing qualitative data. *BMJ: British Medical Journal, 320*(7227), 114.

Porter, M. E. (1980). Industry structure and competitive strategy: Keys to profitability. *Financial Analysts Journal, 36*(4), 30–41.

Skilton, M., & Director, C. (2010). *Building return on investment from cloud computing* (White Paper). US: cloud Business Artifacts Project, Cloud Computing Work Project, The Open Group.

Walther, S., Sarker, S., Sedera, D., & Eymann, T. (2013). Exploring subscription renewal intention of operational cloud enterprise systems- a socio-technical approach. *ECIS Conference Proceedings*. Utrecht, Netherlands.

Wohl, A. (2008). *Succeeding at SaaS: Computing in the cloud*. US: Wohl Associates.

Cloud Computing SaaS Glossary

Application Server Provider (ASP) Business providing computer-based services to customers over a network, such as access to a particular software application using a standard protocol.

Anomaly Detection The identification of unusual data records that might be interesting or data errors that require further investigation.

Attrition Customer attrition, also known as, churn, turnover or defection is the loss of clients or customers at the point of renewal.

Business-to-Business (B2B) It describes commercial transactions between businesses.

Business-to-Consumer (B2C) It is a commercial transaction, which occurs between a company and a consumer.

Business Model The rationale of how an organisation creates, delivers and captures value (Osterwalder and Pigneur, 2010, p. 14).

B2B Applications They 'refer to the use of computerised systems (e.g. Web servers, networking services, databases) for conducting business among different [business] partners' for the purposes of 'procurement, customer relationship management, billing, accounting, human resources, supply chain, and manufacturing' (Medjahed et al. 2003, p.59).

B2C Applications They include virtual malls, customised news delivery, traffic monitoring and route planning for the purposes of engaging with private consumers.

© The Author(s) 2018
D. Dempsey, F. Kelliher, *Industry Trends in Cloud Computing*,
https://doi.org/10.1007/978-3-319-63994-9

Churn See attrition above. In the business context, churn refers to both the customers' migration and to their loss of value.

Churn Rate Percentage of customers who end (full churn) or reduce (partial churn) their relationship with the provider in a particular time period.

Classification Task of generalising known structure, to apply to new data.

Cloud Broker An individual or organisation that consults, mediates and facilitates the selection of Cloud Computing solutions on behalf of an organisation. A Cloud broker serves as a third party between a Cloud service provider and the organisation buying the provider's products and solutions.

Cloud Computing (CC) A model for enabling ubiquitous, convenient, on-demand network access to a shared pool of configurable computing resources (e.g. networks, servers, storage, applications and services) that can be rapidly provisioned and released with minimal management effort or service provider interaction. National Institute of Standards and Technology (NIST) definition in Mell and Grance (2011, p.1).

Cloud Controller It is a storage appliance that automatically moves data from on-premises storage to Cloud storage. Most of the data held on premises is cached for high performance, while less frequently accessed data is moved to the Cloud.

Cloud Service Provider (CSP) It offers customers storage and/or software services via a private or public Cloud (network), normally over the Internet.

Cloud Storage See online data storage below.

Clustering The task of discovering groups and structures in the data that are in some way similar, without using known structures in the data.

Community Cloud A Cloud service model that provides a Cloud Computing solution to a limited number of individuals or organisations that is governed, managed and secured commonly by all the participating organisations or a third party-managed service provider.

Crippleware Client access restricted to a demonstration version of the software; linked to the enticement sales model.

Customer Divestment A strategy to identify those customers who are unprofitable and not of strategic importance to the SaaS provider, with the intent to renegotiate the customer relationship at renewal.

Customer Lifetime Value (CLV) Model It attempts to predict the net profit attributed to the entire future relationship with a customer. Places a monetary value on the customer relationship.

Customer Relationship Management (CRM) Strategy for managing an organisation's relationships and interactions with its current and potential customers.

Customer Retention Ability of a company or service to retain its customers over some specified period.

Customer Service Satisfaction Survey (CSAT) CSAT is a broad term used to describe many different types of customer service survey questions. The goal of any CSAT score is to measure a customer's satisfaction level with a company's product, service or interaction.

Customer Turnover See attrition above.

Data Mining The computing process of discovering patterns in large data sets involving methods at the intersection of machine learning, statistics and database systems.

Decision Support System (DSS) It is a computer-based information system that supports business or organisational decision-making activities, typically resulting in ranking, sorting or choosing from among alternative options.

Demo Ware (trial ware) Client access restricted to a demonstration version of software (see crippleware above); linked to the enticement sales model.

Dependency Modelling Also known as ARL (association rule modelling), dependency modelling searches for relationships between variables.

E-Commerce It is the transaction of buying or selling online.

Enterprise Resource Planning (ERP) It is the integrated management of core business processes, often in real time and mediated through software and technology. Under the SaaS mantel, business activities can include service delivery, marketing and sales, finance.

Enticement Sales Model It encourages subscribers to impulse buy or upgrade their existing service based on restricted services (e.g. linked to Freemium, crippleware and demo ware/trial ware offerings).

5th Utility CC SaaS conceived of as a utility, just like gas, electricity, water and telephony where SaaS is delivered as an elastic and scalable service for which the user pays as the service is consumed (Buyya et al. 2009).

Freemium Built on future revenue expectation (Niculescu and Wu, 2011), the subscriber is offered access to a basic version of the software or for a set trial period for 'free', with the assumption that users will ultimately upgrade to premium use of the full version of the software and/or when the trial period expires.

Generation Z The demographic cohort born after the Millennials. This cohort is also known as Centennials, Post-Millennials, Plurals or the Homeland Generation in the US.

Hybrid Cloud An integrated Cloud service utilising both private and public Clouds to perform distinct functions within the same organisation.

Infrastructure as a Service (IaaS) It focuses on the delivery of technical, service-hosting infrastructure and essentially provides virtual computing resources delivered over the Internet, again as a subscription service. It offers a capability to the consumer to enable them to perform storage, processing and network activities and to avail of other basic computing resources through Cloud technology.

Machine Learning Subset of computer science that gives 'computers the ability to learning without being explicitly programmed' (Samuel, 1959).

Meta-data A set of data that describes and gives information about other data.

Millennials Also known as generation Y, there are no precise dates for when this demographic cohort starts or ends. Demographers and researchers typically use the early 1980s as starting birth years and the mid-1990s to early 2000s as ending birth years.

Net Promoter Score (NPS) NPS is an index ranging from −100 to 100 that measures the willingness of customers to recommend a company's products or services to others. It is used as a proxy for gauging overall customer satisfaction with a company's brand or service and the customer's loyalty to that brand.

Online Data Storage Sometimes referred to as Cloud storage, this refers to the practice of storing electronic data with a third party service accessed via the Internet. It is an alternative to traditional local storage such as disk or tape drives and portable storage such as optical media or flash drives.

OpenSource The end user can use publically available, full function software freely without a licence subscription. While it can have a price tag, it is unlikely that the average end user will incur this cost.

Operating System The low-level software that supports a computer's basic functions, such as scheduling tasks and controlling peripherals.

Platform as a Service (PaaS) It offers a technical service providing both a platform and a development environment. It allows business application developers to build their functional application and service offerings on a pre-proven delivery platform, again providing access to the platform over the Internet. It facilitates deployment onto the Cloud infrastructure of consumer-created or acquired applications created using programming languages, libraries, services and tools supported by the provider.

Predictive Analytics Advanced tools and applications, specifically designed to analyse, in depth, the SaaS provider's customer data, and make predictions based on the information obtained from analysing and exploring that data.

Private Cloud A hosted, single-tenant infrastructure that, although allowing the end user access to the application service as if it were a Cloud Service, is managed and delivered through a single, unique, hosted environment licensed in a model closer to the traditional industry licence than that of the Utility Cloud (Sotomayor et al. 2009).

Public Cloud A multitenant environment, where you buy a 'server slice' in a Cloud Computing environment that is shared with a number of other clients or tenants.

Revenue Model It describes an organisation's revenue flow.

Recurring Revenue The portion of a company's revenue that is highly likely to continue in the future. The potential future revenue associated with current SaaS subscriptions (assuming renewal) is referred to as recurring revenue.

Regression It attempts to find a function which models the data with the least error.

Service-Level Agreement (SLA) A formal commitment that prevails between a service provider and a client specifying service quality, availability and responsibility of each party in the agreement.

Shareware Users are encouraged to make and share copies of the software for free distribution among other users.

Shelfware Software purchased as part of a bundled licence deal. Commonly where volume license prices are given and the B2B subscriber purchases more software than really needed to obtain that discount.

Software as a Service (SaaS) It offers the implementation of specific business functions and processes that are provided with particular Cloud capabilities; that is, SaaS provides applications/services using a Cloud infrastructure or platform rather than providing Cloud features (Frantsvog et al. 2012). It operates based on a software deployment model through which a CC provider offers applications for consumers to use as a service based on their demand (Lewis, 2012), permitting a large number of independent users to simultaneously use the same software application (Barqawi et al. 2016).

Subscriber Customer/consumer/client in the CC SaaS environment.

Subscription Fixed service fee based on usage level/set time period.

Supplier CC SaaS provider.

Version Control A system that records changes to a file or set of files over time so that you can recall specific versions later.

Virtualisation Platforms Keeps the backend and user-level concepts different for each user.

Wiki A website on which users collaboratively modify content and structure directly from the web browser.

Index[1]

---

[1] Note: Page numbers followed by 'n' refer to foot notes.

© The Author(s) 2018
D. Dempsey, F. Kelliher, *Industry Trends in Cloud Computing*,
https://doi.org/10.1007/978-3-319-63994-9

Printed in the United States
By Bookmasters